Royal Botanic Gardens Kew

Witch's Forest

Trees in magic, folklore and traditional remedies

Sandra Lawrence

WELBECK

Introduction

So many images are conjured when someone mentions the word "forest". The lush, Lincoln-green oak woodlands of Robin Hood and his Merry Men. The dripping leaves and dense undergrowth of a tropical rainforest, mysterious, moss-clad branches appearing through the mist of its temperate cousin. A cool, still pine forest, sunlight filtering on to a thick bed of crunching needles. Dappled moonlight shining silver on a silent glade at midnight.

Humans have told stories about trees for as long as they have told stories. Towering above us, the cathedrals of the natural world, they are the planet's tallest living things, often hundreds of years old. They represent strength, longevity, wisdom. The ancients believed that trees have souls, sometimes embodied in supernatural creatures, bound to a specific species, or even a specific specimen. We have learned to use trees in every possible way, for food, warmth, shelter, clothing and medicine, and yet there is still much that we do not understand about these majestic giants.

Our relationship with the wildwood is complex. We need it – for shelter, food, fuel and sanctuary – we hunt in it, walk in it, hide in it, yet even as we do, we are aware that it does not reveal all its secrets. Just as it conceals us, it conceals others, and who knows who – or what – those others may be. Outlaws and cutpurses, spirits and ghosts, wise folk and Gentle Folk (fairies); witches, kindly and otherwise. It would be very easy to get lost in such darkness, never to return.

Writing this book has often been a frustrating experience. Not because there is no folklore, legend or superstition about trees; quite the opposite. Entire books have been written about the legends surrounding a single species, sometimes a single tree. I cannot hope to capture anything but the tiniest crumb from the folktale banquet surrounding woods and forests, and the trees that grow in them. I have hardly touched the myriad life forms, both natural and supernatural, that populate the woods in the human imagination. I can only humbly suggest that this book may act as a springboard to a lifetime of exploration. Hundreds, perhaps thousands of books, articles, stories, legends, superstitions, recipes, spells and histories have been written, spoken and whispered about the forest and its trees. May you enjoy many, many more than I have had room to explore in this book.

Chapter 1:
The Ancient Grove

The forest is one of the world's most ancient sacred sites, equal in age only to the rivers that flow through it and the mountains it cloaks. Nearly every culture has its own version of the sacred grove, and somehow, even in our deforested, concrete modern world, we all retain its image, buried in folklore, half-memory and perhaps even our souls.

The world's sacred groves are of profound religious importance but are also often the last of a community's protected areas, home to rare and endangered plants and animals. Wherever they are, their stories are often remarkably similar.

The ancient Indian Aranyakas (literally "forest books") are a series of four Vedas (religious texts) said to have been written by *rishis* (enlightened scholars) between 700 and 900 BCE. Living apart in forest *ashrams*, or hermitages, the rishis could meditate close to the spiritual wildwood, away from humanity. The concept of a sacred grove is, however, by no means exclusive to sages. Historically, rural communities protected parts of the surrounding forest as dwellings of the gods, though permission was usually granted for the gathering of medicinal plants.

Under colonial rule the system broke down. Ancient village rights were derecognized, and sacred groves considered mere timber. Areas where the tradition survived are often among the most biodiverse habitats on the planet, but even after Indian independence Mahatma Ghandi's fervent pleas to re-empower rural communities were ignored. From the 1980s a series of "save the forest" campaigns led to the Scheduled Tribes and Other Traditional Forest Dwellers (Recognition of Rights) Act of 2006. So far, over 3,600 villages in the state of Maharashtra have regained community rights over their surrounding forests, but there is still a long way to go in replacing India's lost sacred woods.

The ancient Greeks had a nymph for every occasion. Homer talks of the *alsea*, the nymphs of glens and groves and part of Arcadia, a vision of pastoral perfection. Oracles might be divined at such places, such as the oak grove at Dodona in north-western Greece. Priests and priestesses interpreted the whispering of the wind through the leaves, which may or may not have been the wisdom of Zeus depending on whether you are reading Homer, Euripides, Strabo or Herodotus. In the myth of Jason

Below *The Sacred Grove, Beloved of the Arts and Muses* by Pierre Puvis de Chavannes, 1884.

and the Argonauts, the *Argo*, Jason's ship, was capable of similar prophesy because a single timber in its prow came from Dodona.

In northern Europe, Bronze Age and early Iron Age rock carvings often carry tree motifs. At Lunda, a Viking farm on the Swedish coast, archaeologists have discovered burnt sacrificial remains on a hillside, potentially marking it as a sacred wood. *Lundr* is old Norse for "grove", so adding a deity's name – for example Freyr, brother of Freyja – reveals that the glade was dedicated to that god. The modern place *name* Fröslunda translates as "Freyr's Grove".

It is clear from mythology and archaeological excavation that forests were important to ancient Germanic peoples, but the first written account is by the Roman senator Tacitus. His historical ethnography *Germania*, originally called "On the Origin and Situation of the Germans", tells us that the people of the north consecrated woods and groves in the name of specific gods, which they could see "only with the eyes of devotion". Tacitus might have taken a long hard look at his own people. There is no record that Roman pilgrims saw their gods by eyes other than devotion either. The Roman *lucus* (sacred grove) was different from the holy woodlands of the Germans only in that it was cultivated, and often contained a shrine or grotto for travellers to use as a focus for individual rituals such as prayers or offerings to the gods. The *lucus* was separate from other forms of forest: the *silva*, a natural wood, *saltus* (wilderness) and *nemus*, a planted but unconsecrated forest. The *lucus* also had its own feast days: the Lucaria, Festival of the Sacred Grove, which took place on 19 and 21 July. It is unclear exactly what form the celebrations took.

Opposite *Southern Landscape with Classical Ruins* by Ferdinand Knab, 1899.

The Christian Church was very suspicious of the forest and its pagan connotations. King Cnut outlawed tree worship in the eleventh century, though many have pointed out the similarities between the ancient pagan groves and the soaring, tree-like vaulting of the great cathedrals of Europe.

Before the arrival of Europeans, New Zealand's Māori revered as gods the great forests of kauri (*Agathis australis*). These were places to sing and contemplate and tell stories of Father Sky and Mother Earth, locked in passionate embrace. As usual, colonists saw these majestic giants – second in height only to sequoia – as a resource. Today, only a handful survive, solemn and imposing, a reminder from the time of the gods. The two greatest reflect the status they still hold: *Te Matua Ngahere*, Father of the Forest, and *Tane Mahuta*, Lord of the Forest.

A similar story of colonization is told in many African countries, though some of the precious groves have also become degraded thanks to the pressures of poverty, corporate greed and climate change. The remaining groves become sanctuaries for wildlife as well as villagers and in many countries everyone – living, dead and unborn – has a role to play in their protection. Osun-Osogbo Sacred Grove, on the outskirts of Osogbo, south-west Nigeria, is one of the most famous African groves. The dense forest, its meandering river and clearings, are home to the Yoruba fertility goddess Osun. Covered with shrines and carvings it is recognized by UNESCO as having outstanding universal value but is probably the last of its kind in Yoruba culture. Ghanaian groves also often include a stream, and trees known as Nyame Dua ("God's tree", *Vachellia xanthophloea*), which have healing powers to drive away bad spirits and prevent attack by evil. The Akan people of present-day Ghana and Ivory Coast are protected by the goddess

Asaase Yaa, who also lives in a sacred wood. Farming, hunting and even washing clothes anywhere nearby is forbidden, though sometimes the collection of plants for medicine is allowed.

The strange rocks and caves of the Shilin, or Stone Forest, of southern China are a popular tourist attraction, but hidden from the millions of visitors, the sacred Sani groves are places to worship the gods. Like most indigenous peoples, the Sani see their relationship with forests and especially sacred groves as stewardship. The Cultural Revolution saw many of the tallest, oldest trees felled for steel furnaces, and with them the old beliefs teetered. Very slowly, however, the importance of ancient folk traditions is being recognized. Those who have not migrated to the cities are working on community-driven projects to recover the old ways before it is too late, at the same time improving lives and the ecosystem.

A different interpretation of the sacred wood involves the Seven Sages of the Bamboo Grove. Disillusioned with the politics and corruption of third-century China, they retreated to the forest to discuss Daoism, poetry and music and have been depicted in Chinese art and literature since the Ming dynasty (1368–1644). In Japan the Seven Sages motif was used as early as the ninth century.

In Japanese Shinto, *kami* (nature spirits) live in *kannabi*, natural features including woodland groves, rock formations, waterfalls and mountains. *Chinju no mori* are small forests surrounding Shinto shrines that may include kusunoki *(Cinnamomum camphora)*, sugi *(Cryptomeria japonica)* or icho *(Ginkgo biloba)*, roped off with a *shimenawa,* or twisted rice straw, around their trunks. Such groves are marked by a distinctive *torii* gate at the entrance.

Opposite The Bodhi Tree under which Gautama Buddha is believed to have attained enlightenment.

Below The Bodhi Tree with its aerial roots, from *The Infinitely Great and the Infinitely Little*, 1882.

Banyan, Balete and Baodhi

Ficus benghalensis,
Ficus benjamina,
Ficus religiosa

In Polynesia, "Under the banyan tree..." is a traditional fairytale opening, not unlike "Once upon a time..." The phrase harks back to days when storytellers told such tales under the fig tree's capacious canopy.

Many traditions refer interchangeably to the banyan, balete and bodhi (bo) trees, but although they are all in the same *Ficus* family, each is a distinct species.

Banyan (*Ficus benghalensis*) is the national tree of India. It symbolizes the Hindu *Trimurti*: Brahma the creator, who lives in the roots, Vishnu the protector, who dwells in the bark, and Shiva the destroyer, who resides in the aerial roots. In one form, Shiva sits, beneath the banyan, facing south, where lives Yama, Lord of Death, who is also associated with the tree.

The epic *Mahabharata* tells of Savitri who, devastated by the death of her husband Satyavan, lays him under a *vat* (banyan). Impressed by her piety, Yama offers her any boon – except her husband's life. Savitri asks for a thousand sons. Yama realizes he cannot grant the wish without returning Satyavan and concedes defeat. Ever since, married women have tied ceremonial ribbons around a banyan tree during the festival of Vat Purnima in memory of Savitri.

Banyan is also associated with immortality thanks to the constant supply of new roots, even after the mother root has died, giving the tree yet another name: *Bahupada* – "one with many feet". Others call the banyan *Kalpavriksha*, the granter of wishes, wealth and good luck, but other strong beliefs also loom: that demons, spirits and lost souls lurk nearby, especially around specimens in burial grounds. Despite this drawback, the banyan is so beloved that people often compromise by growing the trees as communal meeting places – on the outskirts of villages, just in case...

The bodhi or bo tree (*Ficus religiosa*) – also known as the "sacred fig" and "the tree of awakening" – holds enormous significance for the Buddhist faith, for it was underneath such a tree that Siddhartha Gautama is said to have found enlightenment in the sixth century BCE. The original tree, growing in northern India, is long gone, but in 236 BCE a Buddhist nun took a cutting, which was planted at Anuradhapura in Sri Lanka. Today it is the oldest human-planted tree with a known planting date. A sapling from this tree was then returned to Bodh Gaya, where it grows in the grounds of the Mahabodhi Temple in the Indian state of Bihar.

Opposite Weeping fig tree (*Ficus benjamina*) shown in *The Great Square of Malang, Java* by Marianne North, c. 1876. Kew Collection.

Overleaf Banyan trees (*Ficus benghalensis*) at *Buitenzorg, Java* by Marianne North, c. 1876. Kew Collection.

According to Polynesian folklore, the deity Hina the Watcher lived on the moon for a while, wearing a *tapa* (cloth) made from the bark of a banyan growing there. One day a branch fell from the tree and floated down to Earth. Hina's pet pigeon ate the figs and distributed the seeds across the world. Hina's "moon banyan" was probably a balete tree (*Ficus,* including *F. benjamina*), and this is only one of hundreds of such tales shared across Asia and the Pacific.

The balete is not a "tree" in the purest sense, but a hemiepiphyte. It starts life attached to its host – usually but not always another plant – gaining its moisture and nutrients from the air. As it grows larger, however, it sends down roots to the ground, engulfing its host and gaining a new name: "strangler fig".

Balete trees are perhaps at their most powerful in the Philippines, where they are both visions of wonder and fear. Hiding within the tree might be the supernatural, humanoid spirits *engkantos,* dwelling cheek by jowl with *duendes* (dwarves), *diwatas* (fairies), *kapres* (demons) and *tikbalangs* (bipedal horse-demons). In rural areas people occasionally still leave sacrifices for such beings, but everywhere people treat the trees with respect. On entering a forest they will often excuse themselves by saying *"tabi tabi po"*, just to make sure they will avoid any diseases or bad luck sent by aggrieved spirits.

Several of the most venerable baletes are tourist attractions in their own right, including the gigantic Millennium Tree in Maria Aurora, said to be largest of its kind, or the hollow balete at OISCA farm in Canlaon City, home to lizards and bats and lit by night by a million fireflies. On the "mystic island" of Siquijor, said to be the home of *mambabarang* (witches), a spring gushes from yet another famous balete tree.

Balete Drive in New Manila is named for a spectacular specimen that used to stand in the middle of the road. Since the 1950s various versions of an urban legend tell of a mysteriously veiled white lady who waits beneath a tree by night. After passing her, drivers are said to have looked in their rear-view mirror, only to see her lying, bloody, on the back seat. The story has grown and spread with the internet.

Many members of the *Ficus* family make popular houseplants, but no one in the Philippines brings a balete into the house, for fear of also inadvertently inviting the ghosts that dwell within it.

Opposite Banyan (*Ficus benghalensis*) from *Curtis's Botanical Magazine*, 1906.

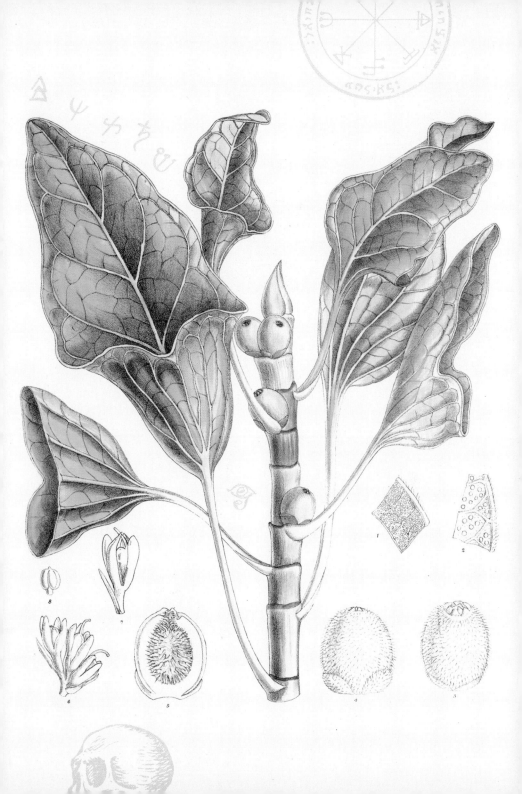

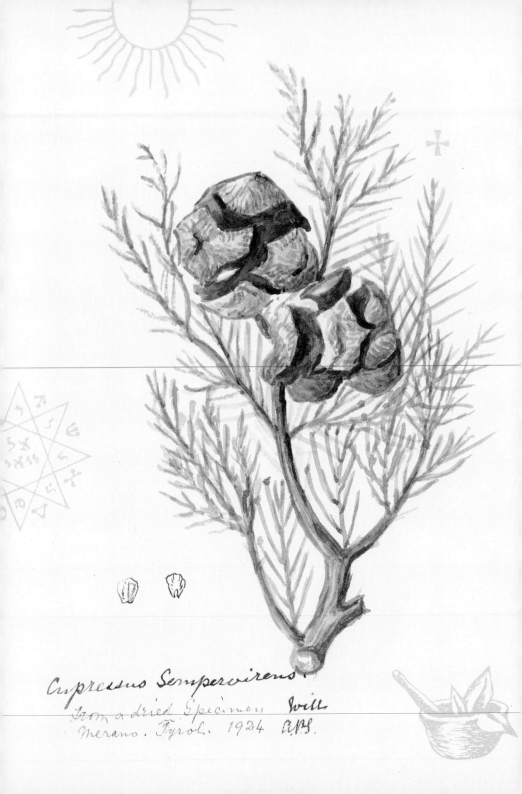

Cupressus Sempervirens

From a dried Specimen. Will
Merano. Tyrol. 1924. A.N.S.

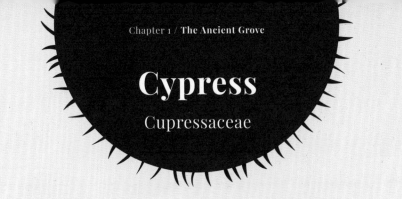

Cypress

Cupressaceae

While the name "cypress" is given to a large group of trees, not necessarily all in the same family, the classic Italian cypress (*Cupressus sempervirens*) has been revered since antiquity.

A familiar sight dotted through the Italian countryside, the tall, dark green spires studded with tiny spherical cones added height and "architecture" to Moorish, Hellenistic and Roman gardens. The Romans practised *ars topiaria* – a dwarfing and shaping technique similar to modern topiary – to keep the trees under control. More often, however, it was considered a funerary plant, and can still be found shading graveyards in southern Europe, a sentinel, evergreen mourner representing eternal life. The association with death goes back much further, however.

In ancient Greek mythology, the youth Cyparissus prayed for everlasting gloom in penance after accidentally killing his beloved pet deer. Apollo turned him into a slim, dark tree, dripping "tears" of sap. Similarly sombre, the goddess Aphrodite swathed herself in cypress to mourn her mortal lover Adonis, who spent half his year in Hades after being gored by a wild boar. The impenetrable Oracle of Trophonius talks of the bright white cypress that grows near a spring in Hades but gives clear advice to the traveller: "Go not nigh." In Persian myth, a cypress by the tomb of the warrior king Cyrus was said to weep blood every Friday.

The association with funerals continued into Victorian mourning "language", victory over death being symbolized by entwined cypress and palm branches. Yet it has also been a useful wood since ancient times. Noah is said to have built his ark from cypress, and it was a favourite roofing material for temples. A famous example is a church at Verucchio, in the Emilia Romagna region of Italy, dating back to 1200. It is said St Francis himself wished to found a new convent. He helped his followers build a fire, but there was not enough wood, so Francis threw his cypress staff into the flames. The next morning it had burst into life among the ashes. He planted the miracle stick and bult a cloister around the tree it grew into. Cypress's association with fire can also be found in Zoroastrian fire-worshipping traditions, probably due to the tree's shape resembling a flame. In more recent times the poor cypress has lost favour as the reviled cultivar *Cupressocyparis* x *leylandii*. When it is planted in unsuitable places, its dense, fast-growing nature has gained the species an undeserved reputation as a nuisance.

Opposite Italian cypress (*Cupressus sempervirens*) by Mary Anne Stebbing, 1924. Kew Collection.

Chapter 2:
The World Tree

An axis between the celestial poles of the world exists in many cultures. The *axis mundi*, where the Earth meets the heavens, may be an invisible pillar upon which the planet spins, a local landmark – perhaps a mountain, lake or rock formation – or some mythical representation. One of the most common of these motifs is the world tree.

The world tree is found in folklore across the globe, from Haiti to Finland, Hungary to India, Japan to Siberia. Stories occasionally refer to a specific tree, now long dead, but whose descendants have been carefully propagated and are still revered. More often they are either metaphorical or invisible to human eyes.

Most have three regions, representing the different realms of the world. The gods live in the highest branches, humans inhabit the area around the trunk, while the roots are the domains of the underworld. Various animals may live there, too. Birds are usually wise, noble and all-knowing. The creatures of the ground and underworld are nearly always evil. The biblical story of Adam and Eve tempted by the snake to eat fruit from the tree of knowledge is a typical example.

Perhaps the most famous world tree is Yggdrasil, the great ash (*Fraxinus*), supporting the nine worlds of Norse mythology. The great eagle at the very top has never met Nídhogg, the dragon that chews Yggdrasil's roots, but the pair hate each other because Ratatoskr the squirrel spends his days running up and down the trunk relaying insulting messages between them. The tree sometimes shivers and groans, foretelling Ragnarök, the end of the world for gods and men.

Persian mythology tells a similar tale, of the haoma tree, also sacred in Zoroastrian culture. Its seeds populate the world with all plants. In some tales the legendary bird Simurgh lives in its branches, while a frog or snake undermines its roots. A tale told by the Tanzania Wapangwa tribe tells of a great war between humans and animals after the world was created. The animals wanted to eat leaves and fruit from the tree of life, created on a termite mound. The humans wanted to keep the sacred tree pure. The humans won but lost for ever the goodwill of the animals.

The ancient Egyptians believed their gods lived in a giant sycamore fig (*Ficus sycomorus*), while the Mayans worshipped a giant blue-green kapok (*Ceiba pentandra*). In Chinese mythology the fusang,

Left Costume sketch for Faunus, a character from Franz Joseph Haydn's opera, *Armida*, 1784.

Opposite Yggdrasil, the sacred tree in Norse mythology. It is at the centre of everything, including the Nine Worlds.

BAXTERS Patent Oil Printing, 11 Northampton Square.

YGGDRASILL,

The Mundane Tree.

see p 492.

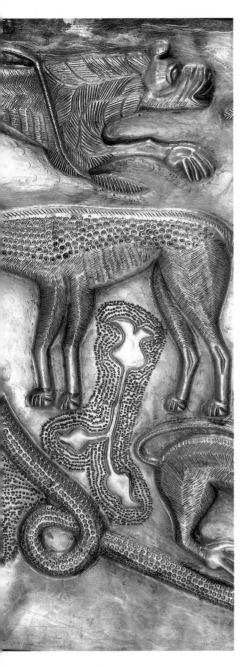

"leaning mulberry" (*Morus*), is the Spirit Tree in which 10 suns used to rest, taking it in turns to climb from the lower branches to the top and back each day. Hou Yi the archer shot nine of the suns out of the sky, leaving just one. In another legend, fusang is also home to a roost of celestial chickens, whose crowing wakes up the poultry of the world each morning.

The oak (*Quercus robur*) is one of folklore's most popular world trees. Lithuanian and Finnish versions are upright, but Baltic and Slavic traditions sometimes invert the image so its branches spread into the ground and roots reach to the skies.

The world tree is a popular North American First Nations motif, embroidered in moose hair and porcupine quills on deerskin garments in Iroquois, Huron and Algonquian cultures. The borders incorporate arches to represent the sky dome, coils for trees and circles as the sun. In Latvia, the mystical oak tree (*Austras koks*) is also used in embroidery, furnishings and folk art. It symbolizes world order and is believed to bring good luck to the wearer.

Left The Gundestrup Cauldron, associated with fertility, abundance and the revival of the dead.

Ash

Fraxinus excelsior

Although most famous for its associations with Norse mythology and the world tree, the ash is also significant in Celtic lore. It is particularly associated with the Welsh mage Gwyddion, whose staff is made from the wood.

One of the great trees of European folklore, the ash may be found from the Arctic Circle to Turkey. It forms a graceful tree with pinnate leaves (three to six pairs of small leaflets, with a single leaf at the end – though in some parts of Britain if you find an even-leafed version it is as lucky as a four leafed clover). The fruits gather into distinctive bunches of "keys" that flutter to the ground on their own "wings". Ash is in the same family as the olive (Oleaceae) and even produces its own "oil".

In ancient Greece humankind was said to have originated from a cloud formed by the Nymphs of the Ash. The name derives from the Old English *aesc*, for spear, and the wood has been used for tool handles and weapons since antiquity. Achilles threw an ashen spear; Cupid twanged arrows of ash. Oddly, the tree was sacred to Poseidon, god of the sea, and in Ireland ash wood was said to be a charm against drowning.

A symbol of paganism, the tree had a tough time with the arrival of Christianity, though people secretly held the ash in esteem and nineteenth-century emigrants carried pieces with them on the long voyage to America.

Negative Christian images of ash persisted. In Scandinavia and Germany, Askafroa, or "Ash Wife"

(Askefrue in Denmark) was an evil spirit who lived inside an ash, and it was whispered that witches' brooms had ash handles. If ash keys failed to appear one year it was believed that a disaster would occur, "proved" by the "fact" that none came in the year Charles I was beheaded.

Eventually the tree's fortunes changed again. It became bad luck to fell an ash, and several traditions hold that snakes will not cross a circle of ash leaves. In Scotland people gave a drop of its sap to babies. In several parts of Britain ash buds placed in a cradle prevented the fairies exchanging your child for one of theirs. Perhaps this is the origin of a more recent, twentieth-century tradition of children taking ash buds to school on Ash Wednesday – any child who forgot a twig could have their feet stamped on by their mates. Ash Wednesday originates from early penitents bathing in ashes at the beginning of Lent but that didn't stop the Christian holy day becoming associated with the tree. Neither did it stop bundles of ash faggots being burned during merrymaking at Yuletide.

Opposite Ash (*Fraxinus excelsior*) from *Herbarium Blackwellianum* by E. Blackwell, 1760.

Fraxinus.

1.2. Blüthe
3.4. Frucht
5. Saame

Eschenbaum
Windholtz.

The Tropical Rainforest

Tropical rainforests occur within 10 degrees either side
of the equator, in regions where there is no dry season.
Vegetation is lush, hot, wet – and full of strange tales.

Due to the speed with which tropical jungle grows, any signs of habitation, however impressive, are rapidly subsumed if they are neglected for even a short amount of time, leading to legends about lost civilizations. The mythical South American golden empire of El Dorado, as told back home by Spanish conquistadors, is hidden by dense jungle and reimagined by Hollywood on a regular basis. Across the world at Angkor, the twelfth-century temple of Ta Prohm was abandoned after the fall of the Khmer Empire in the fifteenth century. It is now one of the most famous tourist sites in Cambodia, presented as it was discovered, complete with gigantic spung (*Tetrameles nudiflora*) roots growing through the walls, doors and columns.

Most rainforest folklore, however, is about the jungle itself, not least its trees. In Indonesia the sugar palm (*Arenga pinnata*) is a young girl, Beru Sibo, who sacrificed herself to save her gambler brother. Turned into a tree, her tears (sap) make sweet wine, and hair (leaves) provides roofing for the villagers. In Javanese mythology, the same tree may also be home to the hideous Wewe Gombel, an initially frightening female spirit who abducts and then cares for children who have been abused by their parents.

Mandioca is the edible root of the cassava (*Manihot esculenta*), a popular food source in Brazil. According to Amazonian legend, it grew from the grave of Mani, the baby daughter of a woman wrongfully banished from her village, who had skin that glowed like the moon, proving her mother's innocence, but who died on her first birthday.

Some say the wide girth of the magnificent lupuna (*Ceiba lupuna*) is a door into an alternative domain, populated by the souls of unhappy people, whose bodies continue in the living world. In Peruvian legend the tree is secretly visited by evil shamans who make incantations against individuals in the community. They slice away parts of the bark and hide a stolen piece of the victim's clothing inside it. The sorcerer's quarry does not at first notice their belly swelling and soon it is too late. The only hope is to find the tree and offer it something better.

Strange tales of the rainforest come and go. The walking palm (*Socratea exorrhiza*), native to central and south America, stands on spooky, stilt-like roots that have led to many – sadly unfounded – stories that the tree roams the forest. But miracles still happen: in 2019 scientists discovered the tallest flowering plant in the world, a 100.8-metre yellow meranti (*Shorea faguetiana*). They are convinced the rainforest shelters even taller marvels.

Opposite *Cascade at Tji Boddas, Java* by Marianne North, c. 1876. Kew Collection.

The Temperate Rainforest

Sometimes known as Celtic or Atlantic, the temperate
rainforest is less well known and possibly even more
endangered than the more familiar tropical rainforest.

Cool, mysterious and equally as lush as its tropical cousin, temperate rainforests are found where there is a lot of rain but little change in overall temperature. They are usually on ocean coasts such as the Pacific Northwest, or in mountainous regions including the eastern Himalayas, but can also be found in small pockets in surprising places. Because they occur in such a wide range of terrains, they play host to an extremely diverse set of ecosystems, each with its own trees and associated legends.

Japan was not affected by the last ice age, meaning that woodlands such as the Taiheiyo Evergreen Forest have been refugia for species otherwise reduced by glaciers. It is not known how long the *tsubaki* (*Camellia japonica*) has grown there, but the "tree of the shining leaves" is revered as the place where the spirits stay when visiting Earth. Japanese people love camellias in the wild, in temple gardens and in graveyards, but do not use them as a cut flower since they are associated with beheading, due to the way their flowers fall after blooming.

The Great Caledonian Forest is a series of fragments of woodland in the Scottish Highlands, rich with tales of King Arthur and the mage Merlin. Nobody knows exactly how large it once was, but the idea of a gigantic, lost wood has never died. It is said that somewhere in Loch Arkaig Pine Forest still lies a chest of treasure smuggled from France in 1745 to support the cause of the Young Pretender Charles Stuart, aka Bonnie Prince Charlie. The loch itself is home to a kelpie, a shapeshifting water spirit in the form of a stallion.

Temperate rainforests are some of the most endangered environments on Earth, but there is hope. One of the most recent to be saved, the Great Bear Forest in British Columbia, only began to recover after people from the Heiltsuk Nation were able to become directly involved in the previously stalled agreements with oil and logging companies. The forest, named for the endangered white Kermode, or Spirit Bear, a black bear with a rare recessive gene that turns its fur pure white, is now the subject of strict environmental regulations, giving the Heiltsuk – and the world – cautious reason for optimism.

Opposite Wistman's Wood National Nature Reserve, Devon, England.

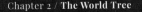

Coconut

Cocos nucifera

The very image of desert island paradise, the coconut is found
in tropical waters virtually worldwide, thanks to the fruit's
remarkable ability to float long distances.

Probably originating in Indo-Malaya, the coconut palm has been revered by humans wherever it has spread. Its large leaves are useful for thatching, its "porcupine" wood, named for its strange quill-like markings, makes furniture, and its tough, weatherproof fibres lash together canoes. It is the fruit, however, that makes the coconut sacred in so many cultures – sweet, juicy and high in fat. Even the shells are useful, making bowls, drums, toys, tools and the buttons on a traditional Hawaiian shirt.

Coconut is a popular offering in south Indian and Sri Lankan temples, burned or smashed on the ground with both hands. The nut was originally introduced as a substitute for human sacrifices to the ferocious goddess Kali because it looked a bit like a human head. Parsee guests break a coconut on the threshold of newly married couples' homes, while in western India, nuts are thrown into the sea to tame the ocean. In Fiji, if you spin a coconut near a sick person and it points east, they will recover.

A Sri Lankan legend – that the first coconut grew from the head of a slain monster – echoes stories told across the Pacific Islands. Many relate to the Polynesian goddess Hina, who became enamoured of an eel that caressed her thighs as she swam. On land the eel turned into the handsome Tuna, King of the Eels. The pair were happy together until a terrible flood threatened the island (location varies, depending on where the story is being told). Tuna told Hina to cut off his head and plant it in the sand. Hina did as he asked, and the floods receded. Green shoots sprouted and grew into the first coconuts whose creamy white flesh is known as *Te roro o te Tuna*, "Tuna's brains".

For Hawaiian people the coconut is a pathway, a bridge between humans and gods, Earth and heaven, living and ancestors. This is illustrated by the Hawaiian spin on the story, where Hina's son asks to meet his father, Ku, who has returned to his homeland. Hina chants to their ancestor Niu (coconut), and a new tree sprouts. The son climbs the trunk, which continues to grow until it bends over, onto Tahiti. The boy and his father make offerings to the tree, and their ancestor appears out of the ocean in the form of an eel to receive their gifts.

Opposite Tucumã (*Astrocaryum vulgare*) and coconut (*Cocos nucifera*) from *Historia Naturalis Palmarum* by Karl Friedrich Philipp von Martius, 1839.

ASTROCARYUM vulgare.   COCOS nucifera.

Chapter 3:
The Stations of the Year

Marking the seasons has always been important to people who live in temperate zones, even within our modern lives. As the world tilts through the year, today's social media threads are filled with photographs of trees swathed in blossom, swirled with leaves, swagged with fruit and, in the dark months, shimmering with snow and ice. Posting such images could be called a modern ritual, reflecting the rites of passage observed by our predecessors.

Recognizing nature's seasons acknowledges the
great stations within our own lives: birth, youth, love,
marriage, childbirth, old age, death.

It is no coincidence that many of the rituals we connect with the stations of the year are closely associated with the forest, the trees standing in for our own lives.

Imbolc (1 and 2 February) is an ancient celebration marking the halfway point between the winter solstice and the spring equinox, although, like all the great holy days, it was later hijacked by the Christian Church. Some believe that Brigid of Kildare, the patron saint of Ireland, is a Christianization of the pagan goddess Brigid. Indeed, the two share a feast day: 1 February. The Christian festival of Candlemas, the blessing of candles to be burned in church, is 2 February. Whatever its name, this is a time for putting darkness away. Anyone foolish enough to have kept sprigs of holly in the house must get rid of them at Candlemas or risk inviting goblins indoors. Outdoors, the days are lengthening, to encourage

the birch (*Betula*), the first-budding tree of spring, to burst into life.

The equinoxes mark the quarter-year, midpoints between the solstices. Nature is at her busiest at the spring equinox, as plants, animals and humans race to utilize the light and warmth. The pagan celebration Beltane is traditionally marked with the lighting of bonfires on 1 May, to welcome the summer. In Scotland farmers drove their cattle around the Beltane fire as a protective ritual, and the younger members of the community leapt over it. May Day is also beloved by the fairies, and it was said a mortal had their best chance of seeing a fairy gathering by creeping around a lone hawthorn bush on May Eve. This behaviour was at their own risk; everyone knew they could be dragged away by the Gentle Folk for such nosiness. Regular May Day celebrations involved a lot of dancing around

Left *Cherry Blossom Viewing
in Mimeguri* by Katsukawa
Shunsen, 1805.

Opposite *Cherry Blossom
Viewing at Uen* by
Katsukawa Shunsen, c. 1781.

maypoles (a tradition possibly harking back to earlier times). After losing popularity during the Industrial Revolution, maypoles were reintroduced in the late nineteenth century with the addition of ribbons and complex dances, instilling in generations of schoolchildren a lifelong hatred of country dancing.

Summer reaches its peak around the solstice, 20 or 21 June in the northern hemisphere, the feast of St John in the Christian calendar. From that moment the year turns. Lammas marks the beginning of the harvest season, a time of toil, but also of plenty, when people spend more time in the fields than the forest. It is the first of three traditional harvests, of grain, hence its origin name, "loaf mass". The second harvest, of fruit from the orchards, traditionally takes place at the autumn equinox, usually around 23 or 24 September, while the third, Samhain, around 31 October, sees the gathering of the last of the hedgerow bounty, such as hazelnuts, sloes, elderberries and damsons. As the end of a long period of hard work, harvest festivals were a joyful exuberance around the night before All Hallows' Day (or All Saints' Day), 1 November.

Samhain was the most important of the fire festivals. Home hearths had been allowed to die during the hard work of harvest, so now people got together for communal fires, often burning wheels as a symbol of the sun and the cycle of life. Cattle that would not make it through the winter were slaughtered, and the feasting was long and loud: everyone knew the winter would be dark.

The last of the year's great festivals once again saw people trudging into the forest, this time in search of a log to burn over the period of the winter solstice, Yule. There was still food left over from harvest, and country folk had little to do in the fields during the short, cold days and longer, colder nights.

Yule and, later, Christmas, allowed them to take time out to light more fires, eat, drink and make merry as a way of sustaining them through the dark days, but they always remembered that the forest was not to be trifled with.

Many of the monsters and bugaboos of Christmas live in the woods. The Austrian Krampus, a demonic goat-creature, emerges from the dark

forest, searching for naughty children, armed with a sack and bird rod. Greek *kallikantzaroi*, malevolent goblins, take time off from sawing down the tree of life to steal children born over the 12 days of Christmas. The Alpine witch, Frau Perchta, will appear either in divine beauty or as a hideous crone who will slit open your stomach and swap your guts for stones. Iceland has many spirits including the evil Christmas cat, Jólakötturinn, and the once-terrifying Yule Lads, now reduced to mere advent pranksters.

All these monsters have one thing in common: they emerge from the forest during the darkest nights of the year. Mortals should beware.

Above *Country Dances Round a Maypole* by Francis Hayman, c. 1741.

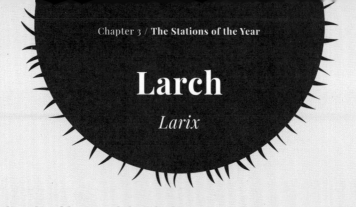

Larch

Larix

Pliny the Elder noted that the largest tree in Rome was a larch, but this would have been highly unusual. In the wild, they are found on rocky, mountain slopes where other conifers struggle to survive.

Despite its being a conifer, larch is deciduous, and loses its leaves in autumn. Its "fluffy" look is down to spirals of fresh green needles each spring, offset by pretty pink clusters of scales. Later these "larch roses" harden and darken into cones, creating a different beauty against the now grey-green needles.

In the Tyrolean Alps, the European larch (*Larix decidua*) has long been considered sacred. A forest spirit called the Salige Frau (blessed woman), dressed in white, sang in the larch wood, made her home in the tree roots and helped humans. Courts of law were held in the shadow of her larch. People left her offerings, and arguing and swearing was forbidden nearby. Anyone damaging the tree would suffer themselves until the wound had healed. In Russia and Ukraine, Khanty people left their gifts in forked trunks. In Yorkshire, England they might have had a shock, however, as country folk there hung a foal's afterbirth on larch branches to bring the animal long life.

Larch is seemingly impervious to fire. Pliny noted it made terrible firewood and was useless for charcoal, but it was very useful for other things. Fire-resistant and water-repellent, it made Roman boats and bridges. If you could get the wood to burn, it was thought to disturb snakes and repel witches. Polish people sealed their doors and windows with larch twigs the day before Walpurgis Night (May Eve), when it was said the witches danced. Slavic people made larch amulets for their children to guard against the evil eye. Shamans of the Tungus people of Siberia hollowed out larch trunks for ritual drums for rituals, while the Algonquin First Nation used American larch (*Larix laricina*) for snowshoes.

Oddly, witches, who were supposed to be scared of the tree, were thought to mix larch resin with basilisk blood, viper skin, phoenix feathers and salamander scales to curse the neighbourhood. Regular folk were more practical. Pliny suggested larch sap was good for toothache. The tradition seeped down through history to medieval times when pulled teeth were hammered into the tree trunk to prevent any more of them rotting. French mountaineers chewed it like gum to fix their teeth into their mouths. The needles sometimes secrete a strange white, sweet substance, lending the tree one of its most enduring nicknames: false manna.

Opposite Larch (*Larix decidua*) from *Köhler's Medizinal-Pflanzen*, 1887.

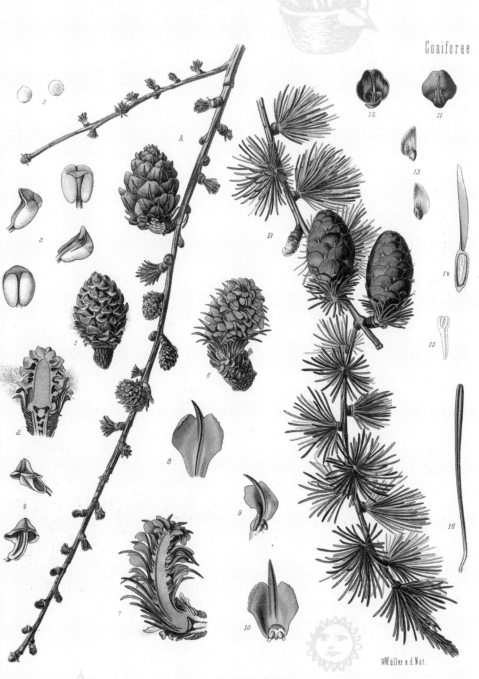

Coniferae.

Larix decidua Miller.

WMüller n. d. Nat.

Imbolc to Beltane

The first few months of the year speak of
optimism, hope and new life. As the trees wake up,
there is much to do, and much to celebrate.

Imbolc (1 and 2 February) marked the halfway point between the winter solstice and the spring equinox. Candlemas now coincided with the first stirrings of spring, when leaf buds swelled. Trees of Imbolc include the willow (*Salix*), traditionally associated with maidens, and rowan (*Sorbus*), also known as the Quickening Tree. Following hard on the heels of birch, the "first" tree of spring, the rowan represents the springing to life of the forest, and sprigs were worn in lapels and hung around the home or cowsheds as protection from evil.

Beltane – 1 May – was a larger folk event than Imbolc. Young people were in the mood for love and the forest in a condition to conceal their dalliances. Beltane fires were lit, with logs of oak (*Quercus*) and birch (*Betula*), and the bravest jumped over them. While King Henry VIII went "a-maying" and held extravagant parties with his courtiers, in humbler circles maypoles were erected on village greens, a Queen of the May chosen and the May King, aka Jack-in-the-Green, processed around town, covered in freshly gathered leaves.

The first known maypole was recorded in 1350, at Llanidloes, Wales. Poles are traditionally made from birch, ash or pine, and people danced around them to the sound of a flute or tabor.

May Day had a dark side, in the form of May Eve, when it was said the witches were abroad. Christians used the excuse of its being the feast of the Christian saint Walpurga to play tricks on each other, drink and make a noise. Beltane is still a joyful festival for modern pagans, a popular time for handfasting, a ritual where the hands of two people are bound together to symbolize the joining of their lives.

Above Townspeople gathering for a maypole dance to celebrate 1 May in the seventeenth century.

Opposite *Henry VIII, Maying at Shooters Hill* from *The Popular History of England* by Charles Knight, 1857.

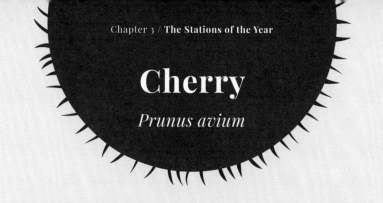

Cherry

Prunus avium

The beautiful blossom of the cherry tree has attracted stories and customs, none more famous than the Japanese tradition of *hanami*, or "blossom viewing".

Television weather forecasters chart the progress of the *sakura zensen* or "cherry blossom front" as the mythical Maiden of Spring flies north, awakening sleeping trees with her warm breath. Most of Japan's ornamental cherries are clones of a single tree, *Prunus* x *yedoensis*, guaranteed to flower together, but many tales are told of individual trees, venerated for their age. The *uba-sakura*, or "milk-nurse cherry", is named for a wet nurse who gave her life for the child she cared for, while the *jiu-roku-sakura*, "the cherry of the sixteenth day", blooms at the same time each year in memory of the samurai who sacrificed himself to save it.

As Japanese people dress in their finest kimonos to picnic beneath the blossom, their national flower becomes a symbol of renewal, its blossom representing the briefness of life. Chinese mythology, however, equates the cherry with immortality, noting that the mythical phoenix sleeps on a bed of cherry petals.

Japanese flower arrangers display the whole cherry stems, considering each component equal in importance, while in the Czech Republic, people bring bare branches home on St Barbara's Day, 4 December, ensuring the dormant buds will flower in time for Christmas.

In European Christian folklore when the pregnant Mary asked Joseph to pick her a cherry, Joseph told her he should ask the father of the child in her womb to do it. In her womb, Jesus bid the cherry to lower its limbs for her, shaming Joseph for his lack of faith.

It is said that New York's Broadway has a famous kink thanks to a tavern keeper, one Hendrick Brevoort, who liked to sit under his cherry tree of an evening and refused to let the road go over its roots. All town officials could do was divert the road around the tree.

Cherry stones are sometimes used in divination, while cherry juice has long been used as a general tonic. Recent research has shown that very large quantities of cherries can lower the levels of uric acid in the blood, proving the folk use for gout to be based in truth. The tree's bark is used by dyers for creams and browns, its roots make a red-purple colour.

The wood of the cherry is hard and fine-grained. In Scotland it was used for bagpipes, and the strange growths or "burrs" often found on cherry trunks were hollowed to make the two-handled "quaich" drinking cup, a symbol of hospitality. The bird cherry (*Prunus padus*) is often thought of as a witch's tree, giving it one of its alternate names, the hagberry.

Opposite Sweet cherry (*Prunus avium*) from *La Belgique Horticole*, 1853.

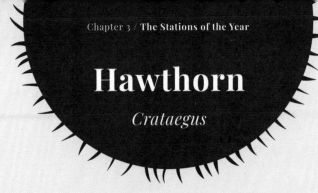

Hawthorn

Crataegus

"Cast not a clout 'til May be out," advises the saying, warning us to keep well wrapped up until summer arrives. Until 1752, this might have meant either the month of May or the blossom named for it.

*C*rataegus is usually known as hawthorn, from the Old English *hagedorn*, or "hedge-thorn", but it has many names. It was often used as a base for hedges because it establishes fast, gaining it another popular name, quickthorn. Until the calendar changed from Julian to Gregorian in 1752, the tree flowered around 1 May, the only day it was not unlucky to bring hawthorn into the house. Going "a-maying" usually involved youngsters bursting into the fresh green countryside to gather the blossom of the "may tree", play pranks or do a little outdoor courting.

Henry VIII loved maying, and his courtiers arranged for "surprises" along the way. One year he met "Robin Hood"; another May morning, Henry burst into Queen Katherine's chambers dressed as the outlaw himself, accompanied by 11 "merry men".

Despite the fun and games, the hawthorn is a spiritual tree, of the fairies. The Gentle Folk are most often found in lone hawthorns in the middle of fields; it is a foolish farmer that fells one. Far better to keep their stock in fields boasting such a tree, and hang hawthorn branches outside the cowshed, knowing the fairies will protect the cattle. In Cleveland a cow's placenta was draped on the tree to transfer health to the newborn calf.

In the 1980s a survey by the Folklore Society revealed the hawthorn as Britain's unluckiest plant. It was said the branches caused accidents if brought into the house; another name for it is "mother-die". Hawthorn became a "monument bush", marking the burial place of unbaptized children, crossroads, burial chambers, springs and wells. Eating the berries was said to fill the mouth with lies; the number of untruths told would be revealed by counting the black bits left in the liar's teeth.

Perhaps hawthorn's unluckiness stems from it being one of many candidates for Christ's Crown of Thorns. Legend says King Charlemagne knelt before some thorns from the holy relic, which burst into flower and the air was filled with fragrance, but was that smell pleasant? Hawthorn blossom is said to smell of death and here, science shows folklore to be telling some truth: the odour is of trimethylamine, a chemical also found in rotting tissue.

Opposite Hawthorn (*Crataegus monogyna*) from *Flora Danica* by Georg Christian Oeder, 1794–9.

Solstice and the Forest

Great prehistoric sites are witness to the store our ancestors set by the longest and shortest days of the year. Sunrise and sunset at solstice has always been a magical time.

Most famously Stonehenge, on Salisbury Plain, marks sunrise on the longest day and sunset on the shortest. Just two miles away, however, another monument marks the prehistoric world's reliance on nature and the forest. Formed of six concentric ovals of wooden posts, the Neolithic site of Woodhenge was surrounded by a bank and ditch that align with the summer solstice sunrise. Archaeological excavation at Durrington Walls, the site of another wooden henge a couple of miles away, suggests that it was built to align with the winter solstice.

The word "solstice" comes from the Latin *sol* (sun) and *sistere* (to stand still) marking two points where the sun reaches its maximum and minimum points in the sky, causing the longest and shortest days of the year, usually 21 June and 21 December, respectively. In many respects the winter solstice traditionally held most cause for celebration. People knew that from that moment, the days would start to lengthen, bringing warmth and regrowth. The summer solstice was equally magical but marked a climax: after this the days would slowly shorten, heralding the darkness.

Some traditions, which may be Celtic in origin, talk of the Oak King and Holly King, twin brothers who rule the seasons. They cannot both rule at the same time and so, according to the teller, one brother either defeats the other or merely falls asleep while the other reigns, with the solstices marking the changeover period. In most cultures, however, these were liminal times; celestial boundaries, not just in time but, possibly, between worlds.

The veil between the earthly and fairy kingdom was considered particularly thin at summer solstice. The Gentle Folk were abroad and wise humans stayed away from their celebrations. Others could not resist entering the forest in the hope of seeing or even joining in with fairy revels, but were careful to show respect. It was important not just to avoid other stranger and more evil creatures in the air that night, but also to take precautions against being forced to stay with the fairies for ever, either by foolishly stepping into a mushroom fairy ring, or by being tricked into eating fairy food.

Really clever mortals might wangle themselves some "fern seeds". Ferns (Polypodiophyta) reproduce via spores, but people in the past assumed the reason they couldn't see any flowers or seeds was because they were invisible. They figured that anyone who could get their hands on invisible seeds might be able to bestow invisibility on themselves. Even Shakespeare thought the idea had merit: "We have the receipt of fern seed, we walk invisible" (*Henry IV, Part 1*). Some went even further, suggesting that discovering such seed or

Top Advert for Liebig meat extract, featuring ancient Germans dancing around a fire at the summer equinox.

Above Advert for Liebig meat extract, featuring ancient Germans celebrating the winter solstice with feasting and song.

flower would render the finder able to understand the birds and animals of the forest, reveal hidden treasure and gain the strength of 40 men.

The magical seed was said to become visible for a very short moment on Midsummer's Eve, and all manner of elaborate ways of collecting it were devised, including placing 12 pewter plates on top of each other – the seed from a magical blue flower would pass through the first eleven and settle on the twelfth. Shooting the sun at midday might work, too: a direct hit would bleed fern seed.

In Slavic traditions, Kupala Night (midsummer) was the only night a fern bloomed. Unmarried women went into the forest bedecked in garlands, searching for the elusive herb, hotly pursued by young men who might not have had fern flowers foremost in their minds. In Sweden, Midsommar is still one of the most important holidays in the calendar. Even

the most urbane city dweller makes for the forests to wear garlands, pick flowers, dance and feast; to make music, make merry and make love.

The winter solstice is an altogether different affair, not least thanks to the difference in temperatures. The one constant between both festivals is fire – the summer fires are lit as purification and to drive away lurking evil spirits. Winter fires symbolize and encourage the newly reborn sun. Fire also marked a crossover between pagan and Christian traditions. At midsummer, British farmers would hang bunches of St John's

Above A print depicting a fire festival in Swabia, Germany from the early nineteenth century.

Opposite A Chinese garden decorated with lanterns and lights to celebrate the longest night of the year.

wort (*Hypericum*) that had been treated with "holy smoke" around the home, cowshed, dairy and even cows' necks to ward off evil.

The Sami people of Scandinavia are so far north that the sun does not even rise on the shortest day. On "Mother Night", therefore, people called on Beiwe to bring her reindeer-driven chariot to the forest and renew the greenery, by making sacrifices and painting butter around their doors to sustain the sun goddess and her reindeer on their journey across the sky. During the Viking solstice

feast of Yule, the Norse goddess Frigg was said to sit at her spinning wheel, weaving the fate of the following year.

In China, the winter solstice Dongzhi is one of the most important festivals of the year. Fruit tree branches used to be cut for divination rituals on the new moon following the winter solstice, and in the northern states, people still count the "Nines of Winter", from an old folk song which explains that spring will come after nine sets of nine days after the solstice.

Aug 17. 1887.

Sycamore
Acer.
pseudo-platanus

Sycamore

Acer pseudoplatanus

One of the reasons why Latin is useful in horticulture is the confusion that can sometimes arise from common plant names. In the sycamore's case, it can be unclear as to which plant various tales and customs are referring.

The biblical story of Zacchaeus tells us the tax collector of Jericho was so keen to hear Jesus preach that he climbed a sycamore, giving the tree its reputation as a symbol of curiosity. This would have been a sycamore fig (*Ficus sycomorus*), not the European sycamore (*Acer pseudoplatanus*) that famously sheltered a group of discontented English labourers in the 1830s. Six of the Tolpuddle "martyrs" were transported to Australia for their rebellion, and their leader, George Loveless, is said to have taken a leaf to remind him of home.

The confusion may come from the European sycamore's deriving from the Greek *sykon*, meaning "fig", for the shape of its leaves, but the Latin name does not help much: *pseudoplatanus* means "false plane". Diarist John Evelyn did not like the sycamore, because its fallen leaves become slippery underfoot. Today, it has gained a reputation as a "weed tree", a thug that smothers entire woodlands, but single specimens can be a stately as any oak, beech or chestnut.

Pliny suggested the root to cure "lameness" of the liver. The tree's tough, light wood was perfect for Roman spear hafts; later the Anglo Saxons made sycamore harp frames, and the wood is still used in violins and pianos.

The Hungarians tell of a king's daughter who went to gather strawberries with her two sisters, who were jealous and took the opportunity to kill her. They buried her under a "maple" tree (probably a European sycamore) before dividing her fruit between them and telling their father she had been killed by a deer. The king was inconsolable, as was a shepherd who had played his flute for her, secretly winning her affections. He passed the tree, noticing a new shoot and fashioning it into a new flute, which he played to the king. The instrument sang a song of the princess's murder in her own voice. The sisters were driven from the castle and the shepherd eased his pain by listening to his beloved's voice as he played.

The sycamore's Old English name, *mapeltrēow*, was first recorded by Geoffrey Chaucer, and the "maple" part of its Acer family can be seen in the sweet sap once drunk by Scottish children. Another old Scottish name, "drool" or "sorrow tree", reveals the sycamore's difficult history. To the 1750s it was the tree of choice for the gibbet.

Opposite Sycamore (*Acer pseudoplatanus*) by Mary Anne Stebbing, 1887. Kew Collection.

Lammas and Samhain

Lammas and Samhain bookmark the three stages of
harvest, a period of traditional plenty, but they also herald
a darkening of the year, and a dying-back of the forest.

Even now there is, just occasionally, new growth. "Lammas flush" manifests in bright green shoots sent out by trees in some years as a response to disease, heat stress, insect erosion or animal damage. The condition is common in broadleaf trees such as oak, ash, beech, sycamore and some conifers, the new growth often tinged with red from protective chemicals produced by the tree to counteract invasion. While there are many customs associated with Lammas, there are few related to trees. This time is for the fields, not the forest.

The second harvest, however, tying in with the autumn equinox, where day and night are roughly equal, brings people into the orchards to gather fruit. Now the apple reigns supreme. The many "Apple Days" celebrated across Britain are a relatively recent invention, but they have roots in the deep past. The ancient Romans celebrated Pomona, goddess of the orchard, on 13 August. In the modern Gregorian calendar this makes little sense, but in the old Julian calendar, Pomona's festival came later, at the beginning of apple season. Cider, pies, apple-bobbing and divination using pips, cores and skins, are all part of the fun.

The Jewish festival of Sukkot is a joyous, week-long celebration of the harvest, celebrated in a tent-like structure known as a *sukkah*. Typically, the sukkah has a roof made from natural branches such as bamboo, pine or palm. "Four Kinds" of tree are carried as part of religious observations: the *etrog* (citron, *Citrus*), *hadassim* (myrtle, *Myrtus*, twigs), *lulav* (palm, Arecaceae, fronds) and *aravot* (willow, *Salix*, twigs).

Far from being an ending, the Celtic festival of Samhain was considered preparation for a new year, and people used bundles of birch twigs to purify their homes and sweep away the spirits of the old season, ready for new things to come.

Two other trees are bound to the festival. Elder (*Sambucus*) is the tree of the crone, the third incarnation of the Triple Goddess (the other two being the maiden, associated with spring, and the matron or mother of the summer). The yew is a symbol of death and rebirth being ancient, hollow, and yet evergreen. Its message is clear, and positive: the year may be dying, but life will go on.

Opposite *Witches Ride*, sketch by J. Copland from *Witchcraft and Superstitious Record in the South-Western District of Scotland* by J. Maxwell Wood, 1911.

Overleaf George Cruikshank's painting of *Herne's Oak* from about 1857 shows people being punished by fairies in the forest.

Elder

Sambucus nigra

One of the most ancient European figures goes by many names. Whether Frau Holle, Holde, Holda, Perchta, Frau Gauden or Hilde-Moer, the Mother of Elves is not to be trifled with, and nor is her tree.

Hilde adores the elder, and indeed she often turns herself into one or, in Denmark, lives in its roots. No one knows which individual tree is the goddess, so it is essential to show respect for your elders.

A self-sown elder is lucky: Hilde has chosen to live in that spot. Elder likes marshy, swampy ground, and was often planted near privies, where it could enjoy the rich damp soil. It repaid its host by keeping flies at bay with a natural insecticide in its leaves. Elders were also planted next to bakeries to deter the Devil.

As the Christian Church suppressed the old gods, Hilde was pronounced "evil". It was said that Judas Iscariot hanged himself from an elder after betraying Christ. Worse, Christ's cross was, apparently, made from elder, after which the tree was so ashamed it shrank to the size of a bush, drooping in shame. Its cursed fruits shrank to tiny berries and its blossom stank of rotting corpses. By the thirteenth century the famous hagiography, The Golden Legend, a compilation of the traditional stories about the saints, called the elder the "Tree of Death", fit only for hanging criminals. When burning, elder wood "spits" and "screams" (due to its hollow stems and exploding globules of sap), so, naturally, adding it to the grate invited the Devil down the chimney.

Regular people never stopped loving the elder. Travellers carried sprigs to protect them from footpads, farmers hung elder crosses over cattle stalls to protect their cows. Elder amulets warded off St Anthony's Fire, while sailors' families kept an eye on the tree outside their homes; as long as it flourished, so did their sons. Elder could fend off snakes, remove poison, cure warts, calm nerves and cure toothache. Anyone nurturing an elder would be sure to die in their own home. In the Tyrol, elder crosses were placed on the graves of loved ones. If the wood bloomed, they had been blessed.

Such benevolence demanded respect. It was essential to ask permission to cut it. The would-be feller had to explain why the wood was needed and to wait for the tree's consent (which was usually silent). Small children were taught to ask the tree politely even for flowers and berries. The reward for politeness was useful wood, food and medicine. The punishment for disrespect was a series of misfortunes. Why take the chance?

Opposite Elder (*Sambucus nigra*) from *Getreue Darstellung und Beschreibung der in der Arzneykunde Gebräuchlichen Gewächse* by F. G. Hayne, 1816.

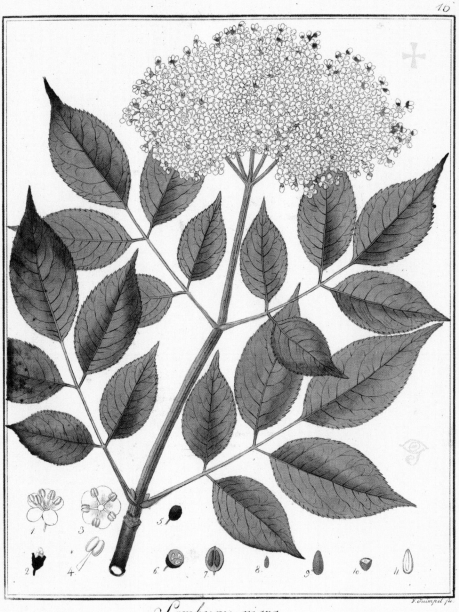

Sambucus nigra.

Christmas Tree

Northern Europe and Scandinavia specialize in winter legends, decorations and customs, but one tradition has spread across the world, transcending seasons and even faiths as a symbol of December festivity.

There are many, many tales surrounding the Christmas tree, perhaps because it has played such a pivotal part in winter festivals for so long. It was, famously, popularized in Britain by Queen Victoria's consort Prince Albert in 1848, but his was not the first British Royal Christmas tree. A homesick Queen Charlotte, wife of King George III, had been brought up to decorate yew branches her home country of Mecklenburg-Strelitz (now part of Germany). At first she continued to do so too, but in 1800 she brought an entire tree indoors, sparking a craze among the British gentry.

In 350 CE, Pope Julius I set 25 December as "Christ's Mass", but many still preferred to decorate for and celebrate the winter solstice than attend solemn mass. In 575 CE, a frustrated Archbishop Martin of Braga, in what is now Braga in Portugal, outlawed decorations of greenery in households. He was, it would seem, largely ignored.

The old faiths needed to be further demonized, even to the point of suggesting human sacrifice. Old tales tell of St Boniface who was sent by Pope Gregory II in the mid-750s to convert the pagans in Hesse, Thuringia, Westphalia and Saxony, all now in modern Germany. He was horrified by a group of pagans worshipping a great oak tree, preparing to make a blood sacrifice to Thor, and took an axe to the tree, sending it crashing to the ground. Noticing a humble fir tree behind it, unharmed by the fallen oak, he pronounced it to be holy, Christlike in its simplicity.

According to another legend, religious reformer Martin Luther brought a small fir tree home for his children and covered it with candles after being inspired by stars sparkling through branches on a Christmas Eve walk. The first written evidence of a Christmas tree, however, is in a Strasburg document from 1605, which mentions people bringing fir trees into parlours and decorating them with paper flowers, apples and sweets.

Back in Britain, Prince Albert's Christmas tree, which so delighted the *Illustrated London News*, was not a surprise to his wife. As a 14-year-old, Princess Victoria had already written in her diary about a similar tree in 1833, lit with candles and hung with almonds, raisins and wax dolls. Crown Princess Helene of Mecklenburg-Schwerin had introduced

Opposite The Christmas tree in Washington, DC in 2020 at night.

a Christmas tree to Paris in the late 1830s and Hessian mercenaries had brought Christmas fir trees to America as far back as the American War of Independence. It was the image of the whole Royal family enjoying the tree that captured the nation's imagination in 1848. Suddenly everyone wanted a Christmas like theirs. The craze reached the United States around the same time as it hit Europe and the first commercial Christmas trees were sold in New York in 1851. The idea received presidential blessing in 1856 when a tree was erected at the White House.

The first tree ornaments were nuts and fruit, biscuits and bows, but by 1850 Charles Dickens was describing trees covered with dolls, "real watches" and jolly figurines filled with sugar plums. The glassworks of Lauscha in the Thuringian mountains, established in 1597, are famous for two things: glass eyes and Christmas baubles. The first glass decorations were made by a poor glassblower who could not afford apples to hang on his children's tree, so he made his own. Or at least that is the story one F W Woolworth told his American customers from 1879 after he started importing thousands of them. In reality, Hans Greiner, a descendant of Lauscha's first glassworks owner in 1597, developed the process in 1847, using a unique system of mouth-blowing and fancy moulds to create fabulous, iridescent shapes, snapped up by Christmas fans. Woolworth's annual buying trips to Germany, along with his sales techniques including "stories" behind the various baubles, set in motion a multi-million-dollar holiday industry. Wax tapers were fastened to branches with wire until the decorations industry invented counterbalances in 1867 and spring clips in 1879. Trees became even brighter in the 1880s with the introduction of electric fairy lights.

There is no set species or variety for Christmas trees. Douglas fir (*Pseudotsuga menziesii*), Fraser fir (*Abies fraseri*), Nordmann fir (*Abies nordmanniana*) and Norway spruce (*Picea abies*) are all popular commercially, but Christmas trees are not always pine, spruce or fir. Some believe the earliest was a palm, with 12 leaves symbolizing the apostles.

Whatever its form, the Christmas tree is much loved, either in the home or as a "community" tree. Some are annual gifts between nations. The Trafalgar Square tree, for example, is sent to the people of Britain from the people of Norway in thanks for help in the Second World War. Others, like the Rockefeller Center tree, first erected in 1931 by construction workers grateful for a job in Depression-hit America, are there for sheer loveliness. Whatever their stories, all Christmas trees bring joy to the world in a time of year often filled with darkness.

Opposite Queen Victoria, Prince Albert and their children gather around the Christmas tree at Winsor Castle in 1848.

The Green Man

The grotesque "foliate heads" carved into corbels, pews, roof-bosses and misericords may only have been named as invocations of the "Green Man" by Lady Raglan in 1939, but the style dates back to the very earliest churches.

The traditional image of a strange face peering out from or even made of dense foliage seems to transcend either pagan or Christian beliefs.

The Green Man (and, less often, Green Woman) can be found in many forms. The earliest representations are on Mediterranean Roman tombs, and the style was incorporated into early Christian architecture, including Byzantine mosaics. It is possible to follow the history of these enigmatic faces along the pilgrim routes from Santiago de Compostela in Spain to Britain via France. They may be of wood or stone, have leafy hair and beards or even spew foliage from their mouths. They may be young or old, or a combination of both, probably representing the cycle of life and regeneration of the seasons.

Sometimes the Green Man is born and grows old in a single church, as with the mysterious Rosslyn Chapel in Scotland. Authors Mark Oxbrow and Ian Robertson discovered that Rosslyn's foliate heads "age" as you move clockwise round the building, starting as fresh-faced boys in the east where the day dawns, and ending as skeletal masks in the north where the sun sets. Yet the true domain of the folkloric Green Man lies outside the church doors – in Rosslyn's case, the dense woodlands of the ancient Rosslyn Glen. Here, like so many north-European deciduous forests, the air seems thick with magic. One could almost imagine being watched.

Thomas the Rhymer is not a Green Man, but in Scottish legends he spends seven years with the Queen of Elfland after meeting her under the Eildon Tree, where she has appeared to him dressed entirely in green, a rare example of a Green Woman. In several French legends, the Devil himself dresses in hunter's green, indicating that he is chasing souls to drag to hell, perhaps even for sport. Green was worn by hunters as disguise, and one of the most famous legendary forest hunters lives in Windsor Great Park, Berkshire. It is said that the antlered ghost Herne the Hunter haunts the spot under an oak where he hanged himself. The story dates back to at least 1597, as Herne is a pivotal plot device in Shakespeare's *The Merry Wives of Windsor*, but there are echoes of him in far older stories. He has been identified by various scholars as the horned Celtic god Cernunnos, as Wotan, an Anglo-Saxon form of the Norse god Odin, or even as a real individual, Richard Horne, who was caught poaching during the reign of Henry VIII.

Another great poacher, often associated with the Green Man, is the outlaw Robin Hood. The legend took a long while to reach Hollywood, but Robin and his Merry Men are now perennial favourites, dressed in Lincoln green and stealing from the rich to give to the poor. Robin is first mentioned in the Sloane manuscripts in the British Museum, written in 1377, but even the earliest chroniclers cannot decide exactly who he was or even if a "real" Robin ever existed. He was an extremely popular figure almost from the outset, however, appearing in plays and ballads and hundreds of local stories throughout England. A man of the forest, he used its cover as a base for insurgency against hated authority figures of the day. His most famous lair is within the mighty Sherwood Forest, his most famous foe the Sheriff of Nottingham, but Robin does not always live in the Midlands – and neither is he the only folk hero of the region.

No one knows who wrote *Gawain and the Green Knight*, one of the most famous tales of King Arthur, but it was probably written in the Midlands in the late fourteenth century. The Christmas feast at Camelot is interrupted by the arrival of a strange and terrifying giant. Dressed in green, with green skin, hair and beard, he carries a holly-bob (staff) of greeting in one hand and an axe of challenge in the other. The stranger dares any knight to strike off his head, on condition that one year and a day later he should have his own removed in the same fashion at the Green Chapel. Sir Gawain takes up the axe and beheads the "green man" with a single blow, then watches, stunned, as the giant picks up his head and leaves. Gawain spends the next year searching for a mysterious Green Chapel in the woods to complete his peculiar quest.

More recent folklore has combined elements from all these characters – and dozens more, including the trickster fairy Puck, ancient Egyptian god Osiris, and even, some have argued, the half-human, half-serpent Nagas of Hindu, Jain and

Buddhist mythology – to create new incarnations and interpretations of the Green Man. Among these are the Oak King of summer plenty and the Holly King who rules the winter landscape. These figures often feature in new or revived customs, such as Jack-in-the-Green, who, on May Day, dances through towns including Rochester, Hastings and even as far afield as Mylor, south Australia, and the Holly Man, who arrives at Shakespeare's Globe in London on Twelfth Night, bedecked in evergreens, to wassail the winter.

Above A woodcut from *The Regal and Ecclesiastical Antiquities of England*, 1793, showing the mythical hairy wild man.

Chapter 4:
The Managed Forest

Historically, the word "forest" was a legal term, for land set aside for hunting by the monarch, and did not necessarily mean "woodland". It could just as easily be a heath, moor or open ground. It was against the law for commoners to exploit, cultivate or even encroach upon vast tracts of countryside declared "afforested" by Royal Decree. That does not mean that nobody did.

The word "forest" may come from the Latin *foris*, meaning "outside". This land was off limits; anyone caught poaching was outside common law, subject instead to specific forest law, where poachers became "out-lawed".

The concept of forest as a legal entity is first mentioned around the ninth century at the court of Charlemagne, for the protection of game. The idea came to an unimpressed England with William the Conqueror. Successive monarchs seized more and more "Royal Forest" until a group of barons rebelled. Famously, they forced King John to sign the Magna Carta, which "disafforested" much of the Royal land-grab.

In 1217 the Charter of the Forest, a supplementary document to the Magna Carta, allowed some rights to people living in Royal Forests. Verderers' courts were established – indeed, a few still exist, as in the New Forest, Hampshire. Offences were now either against game ("venison")

or vegetation ("vert"). Anyone caught committing crimes, including clearing trees, carrying bows or spears, enclosing land or stealing deer, faced the harshest penalties. Documents from Sherwood's Forest Eyre Court, dating from 1287 to 1334, record the crimes of outlaws including Hugh of Wotehale, William Hynde and Wilcock, a former servant of the parson of Clifton. Alas, Robin Hood is almost certainly a myth, but Sherwood had its own, real-life outlaw-at-large, Roger Godberg (sometimes Godberd) whose exploits included murder, violent crime, arson and stealing from the rich, and not much giving to the poor. Elsewhere Eustace the Monk, who menaced the high seas and the forests of Boulogne with his own brand of outrageous and scatological crime, sounds

suspiciously like a candidate for the folk figure Friar Tuck.

"Free men" were granted some restricted rights, such as allowing their swine to forage the forest floor (pannage), collect small twigs (estover; for firewood, not profit) and cut turf for fuel (turbary). Gradually the laws eroded; execution for poaching

Opposite *Harvesting Acorn to Feed Swine* from the *Queen Mary Psalter*, c. 1310.

Above A detail painted by Herman de Limbourg from *Belles Heures*, showing a herd of pigs foraging for acorns, c. 1405.

was commuted to castration or losing a hand or an eye and, by Tudor times, forest laws mainly extended only to specific Royal forests.

That did not mean forests became common land. They were still "owned", mainly by the aristocracy, who also hunted in them but recognized that trees and their various products were highly profitable.

Systematic forestry began in Germany in the sixteenth century when woodlands were divided for timber harvesting on a rotational basis, to ensure yields remained sustainable, and the system quickly spread across Europe. Different species of trees were planted with an eye to the kinds of timber or other products they might produce. Oak (*Quercus*), for instance, was ideal for building, while the rot-resistant properties of the elm (*Ulmus*) made it perfect for barges and water pipes.

Coppicing (from the French *couper*, "to cut") allowed stewards to have their tree and use it too, taking advantage of the natural propensity for many hardwood trees to attempt to regrow after being felled. Allowing shoots to grow from the stumps, verderers could harvest thin, whippy growth for basketry or fencing; older, taller poles for stakes and posts. Alternatively, they could wait until the shoots grew large enough for construction timber.

Coppiced woodlands usually comprised a variety of trees to fill different purposes. Older "copses" were irregular and varied; anything from the nineteenth century tended to be evenly spaced like a plantation. Foresters would retain one or two naturally mature trees to provide some shelter and encourage coppiced shoots to grow straight up towards the available light. The rest of the coppices were managed at different stages of growth for a constant supply of variously sized wood. Willow (*Salix*) was often cut after a year; oaks could take anything up to 50 years to harvest. The stump or "stool" could be many centuries old – older, indeed, than a regular tree of the same variety – and hosted its own micro-ecosystem of mosses, small plants, insects and larger creatures.

Some trees were pollarded, a technique similar to coppicing but allowing the tree to grow a trunk before being lopped, keeping delicate shoots out of the reach of grazing animals.

The other great folk image of the forest is the mysterious, solitary charcoal burner. Charcoal burned much hotter than regular firewood, but to create it required immense care. Colliers lived apart from regular folk, in tents or shacks, deep in the forest, discernible only by wisps of smoke curling from the treetops. Their craft was highly skilled; to the outside world it was arcane, almost alchemical. Their faces and clothes were blackened with soot from tending the furnace. Many villagers wondered what else they did in the woods, who else they consorted with. From medieval times charcoal burners were ostracized, accused of snaring rabbits, pheasants and the odd deer, of drunkenness and even, occasionally, of murder. Some said charcoal burners kept snakes as pets, though in reality the adders attracted to the warmth of a charcoal clearing were hazardous to a collier. For all their "suspicious behaviour" burners may also have been the first people to discover the absorptive and purifying qualities of charcoal, as they dropped pieces of blackened wood into their kettles and cooked it with meat to remove the smell and taste of smoke.

Many old forestry methods, including pollarding and coppicing, are being brought back into use today as ecologically sound ways of managing ancient woodland. Even colliers are returning, as exhausted city folk venture into the woods to burn charcoal instead of their dreams.

Opposite A wood engraving of poachers being caught in the woods, c. 1888.

Spanish Chestnut

Castanea sativa

Forever associated with being roasted on open fires at Christmas time, the charred smell of hot baked chestnuts is as familiar a memory as the fingers burned trying to eat them too quickly.

In antiquity, Spanish or sweet chestnut was known as the Sardian nut, from Sardis, capital of Lydia, now in modern Turkey. Chestnut's scientific name, however, comes from Castanis, in Thessaly, Greece. Theophrastus wrote that the slopes of Mount Olympus, home of the gods, were clad in chestnut trees which, being of the highest quality, were dedicated to Zeus. The Greeks distributed this extremely useful plant across southern Europe and North Africa, then the Romans took over, spreading the chestnut tree across northern Europe. It is easily spotted for its long yellow catkins and fruits whose tasselled husks make it look almost "fluffy". Do not be fooled. Those prickles are sharp.

Chestnut is best farmed as a coppiced tree, sending out shoots that are reliably straight, long and tough. Pit props, stakes, vine supports and fences lasted well thanks to chestnut's rot resistant properties. Leftovers were kiln-baked for exceptional charcoal. High levels of tannic acid found in chestnut made it important to the leather industry but had more underhand uses too. Eighteenth-century smugglers adulterated consignments of contraband tea with chopped-up chestnut leaves.

For most people, however, chestnuts are all about eating. From street-sold paper bags filled with blackened shells, cross-cut to prevent explosions, through starchy flours and rich stuffings to France's elegant marrons glacés, the chestnut's nutritious bounty has been enjoyed for millennia.

In 1911, American writer Charles Lippincott noted the American chestnut (*Castanea dentata)* was eaten on St Simon's Day (9 September) and distributed to the poor on St Martin's Day (11 November). Early colonists copied First Nations people, making cough remedies with chestnut leaves and poultices against poison-ivy rash. Country folk stuffed mattresses with dry leaves, creating "talking beds" that rustled and crackled as the sleeper moved.

In the early twentieth century, chestnut blight (*Endothia parasitica*) caused severe tree loss across both North America and Europe. Many years of work have stabilized the population, but the situation is constantly monitored.

Sweet chestnut leaves are high in tannins, and decoctions made from them have been widely used in folk medicine for centuries, treating respiratory diseases, coughs, colds and asthma.

Opposite Spanish or sweet chestnut (*Castanea sativa*) from *Köhler's Medizinal-Pflanzen*, 1887.

Cupuliferae
(Fageae)

Castanea vesea Gaertn.

T. 2. Nᵒ 14.

ÆSCULUS hippocastanum   MARRONIER d'Inde. *pag.* 54

P. J. Redouté *pinx.*   *Micelle l'ainé Sculp.*

Horse Chestnut

Aesculus hippocastanum

Despite clear similarities in leaf and fruit, the sweet chestnut (*Castanea sativa*) is unrelated to the equally beloved horse chestnut. The fruits of the horse chestnut are not edible, but that does not stop armies of small children gathering them each autumn.

Horse chestnut husks are, like their sweet namesakes, spiky: bright green, miniature land mines. Inside, the fruits gleam like freshly polished satinwood. Even adults find it hard to resist returning home with their pockets filled with conkers.

Mature horse chestnuts are magnificent sentinels, growing to around 40 metres in height and living around 300 years. Each leaf consists of between five and seven jagged leaflets growing from a single stem. In April and May the flowers, often referred to as "candles", range from white to red. Horse chestnut is native to the Balkan Peninsula and was introduced to Europe from Turkey in the late sixteenth century. It has become common in parks and on village greens but, like many large trees, has been waning in popularity as a town tree as gardens become smaller and pavements more crowded.

Chestnut wood is soft, so best for carving. The fruits were traditionally used in horse medicine, hence their name, and the chemical compound aescin, which can be extracted from conkers, does indeed have an anti-inflammatory effect on bruises and sprains. The fruits have long been additives for shampoo, and enterprising Victorian housewives even tried making conker "flour", grinding them up and leaching them for hours to remove the bitterness. One persistent folk-use is leaving conkers in dark corners to ward off spiders. There is no scientific basis for this, but they do contain a chemical compound, triterpenoid saponin, which could, potentially, deter moths.

The first mention of a conker match – a playground battle using chestnuts threaded onto strings – was held on the Isle of Wight in 1848, taking over from similar games played with snail shells and hazelnuts. For a century or so children developed sneaky ways of making their chestnut-on-a-string hard enough to smash their opponent's version. Baking in vinegar or a coat of nail varnish hardened the conker but could make it brittle and more likely to shatter first. The game is losing popularity these days thanks to health and safety concerns, and the tree is also in trouble: from a critter, the horse chestnut leaf miner, and a disease, bleeding canker, both of which threaten one of the most majestic sights of the summer.

Opposite Horse chestnut (*Aesculus hippocastanum*) from *Traité des Arbres et Arbustes* by Duhamel du Monceau, 1804.

The Spinney and the Bosket

William Kent, Humphry Repton and Capability Brown all
knew the power of a well-placed spinney, a favourite weapon
in the eighteenth-century landscape architect's armoury.

"Spinney" is an ancient term for a small wood or copse. Not all spinneys are artificially created, but they often involve ornamental clumps of trees, created as eyecatchers or provide shelter for game birds in a country landscape. Over the centuries, they have naturalized and acquired mystical qualities.

Some spinneys have grown on top of ancient burial mounds or ritual sites. The Rollright Stones, a neolithic stone circle in Oxfordshire, carry legends of an army turned to stone by a witch, herself turned into an elder tree. If the tree is cut down the spell will be broken, but everyone knows the dire consequences of felling an elder and no one has ever dared. It is whispered that the constituent group of stones called the Whispering Knights leave their conspiracies at midnight to drink at the stream in Little Rollright Spinney.

"Wetting the cuckoo" was a nineteenth-century custom among Shropshire labourers who would down tools on hearing the first cuckoo of spring, and rush to whichever spinney in which it had been heard to drink ale and toast its welcome.

Ornamental woods, or *boscos*, surrounded Italian Renaissance gardens as a reminder of the natural world constantly threatening to invade civilization. Built in 1547, the mannerist *Sacro Bosco*, the "Park of the Monsters", at the Villa Orsini in Lazio, pokes gentle fun at the serious nature of such gardens.

Its great forest conceals grotesque sculptures of dragons, hideous faces and mythological beasts dragging the visitor into a strange hell-like fantasy.

Baroque France saw the formal *bosquet*, groups of at least five identical trees, evenly spaced in straight lines. The English "bosket", however, had a much wider interpretation. While sometimes formalized, it often took the form of a contrived "wilderness", suggesting classical ideas of Arcadia.

Some landscaped forests included ornamental "hermitages": grottoes or cabins supposedly lived in by lone, mystical anchorites. Advertisements placed in newspapers for would-be hermits had mixed results. At Hawkstone Park in Shropshire in the 1700s, "Father Francis" sat in pious "contemplation" at a table of skulls, hourglasses and a globe and was so popular that the Hill family had to build an inn to cater for his visitors.

The "recluse" installed in a woodland hermitage by the Hon. Charles Hamilton at Painshill in Surrey, however, was sacked for carousing in the local pub just three weeks into his seven years of contracted solitude. It is no wonder that some estate owners dispensed with humans altogether and installed automaton "hermits" instead.

Opposite *Landscape with a Hermit* by François Boucher, 1742.

Holly

Ilex

As the leafy cloak of yellow and brown falls from summer's shoulders, the Oak King's power falters and the Holly King arrives to rule the winter months. Both are incarnations of the legendary Green Man and in the wintertime, holly bears the crown.

There are over 500 species of the *Ilex* genus, but the most famous, *Ilex aquifolium*, is at its most luxuriant in the British Isles. Another name, "holm", is from the Old English *holen* or *hulver*, meaning "prickle". Being evergreen, (a boon granted the plant after it concealed the infant Christ from Herod's soldiers) it has been used in winter celebrations from Roman Saturnalia through Solstice and Yule to Christmas (a Christian tradition says it concealed the infant Christ from Herod's soldiers).

Bringing holly into the house too soon invites bad luck, especially in Wales where it predicts family arguments. The exception lies with Advent wreaths in churches, symbolizing Christ's death and rebirth. Originally white, holly berries were stained forever crimson by Christ's blood after it was used in the Crown of Thorns. Each Advent Sunday one of four red candles is lit. The final white candle is lit on Christmas Day itself. Wearing a holly sprig to midnight mass, however, risks the double-sided curse of foresight – do you *really* want to see which of your fellow parishioners will die in the coming year?

In Scotland, branches from the "Gentle Tree" were thought to protect humans from fairy mischief during Hogmanay, especially if a gift, usually a silver coin, was left at the tree's base. It is bad luck to keep holly indoors after Twelfth Night. In Devon even a single missed leaf invites goblins, though some keep a single piece until Candlemas, 2 February. A leftover sprig, in a cowshed or beehive, protects the cattle and reminds the bees to sing.

In Norse and Celtic mythology holly is sacred to Thor and Taranis, gods of thunder. A holly tree outside the front door will protect the house from thunderstorms, fire and the evil eye. It is considered effective against lightning, perhaps because while any tall tree may divert a strike, each tiny holly spine can also act as a miniature conductor, bringing Thor's wrath safely to Earth.

Every part of the holly is toxic but folklore still finds it indispensable. Leaves were burned like incense to strengthen magic and a holly wand added protection to a practitioner while performing magic.

Cutting holly courts bad omens, so hedgerows are often punctuated by tall trees, preventing witches from dancing along the top: "dancing" also means "crossing" and "meeting", so uncut holly prevents witches moving across fields to gather.

Opposite Holly (*Ilex aquifolium*) from *The Universal Herbal* by Thomas Green, 1816.

ILEX   AQUIFOLIUM ___ *Common Holly.*

Coniferae.

Juniperus communis L.

W.Müller n.d.Nat.

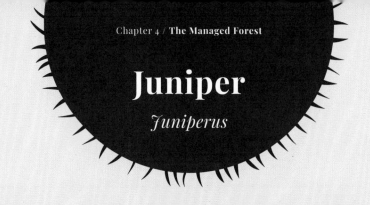

Juniper

Juniperus

"Genever" was popularized in Britain by the Dutch king William of Orange in 1688. Today, gin is one of the world's top selling spirits. Without juniper, however, the drink known variously as "mother's ruin", "ladies delight" and "knock me down" would just be plain alcohol.

The symbol of the fertility mother goddess Asherah in Sumerian and ancient Semitic texts, the sprawling, tortured juniper shrub appears in the Old Testament sheltering the prophet Elijah from evil Queen Jezebel. In the New Testament it becomes another hiding place, for the Holy Family, escaping from King Herod's soldiers.

For the ancient Greeks, juniper belonged to the Furies, goddesses of vengeance. Priests burned the wood to fumigate houses after a death (medieval people did the same during plague times) and the berries at funerals to ward off evil spirits. Later, aromatic juniper smoke was thought to aid clairvoyance and help contact the dead. Burnt in spring rituals juniper expelled witches, though in Scotland it usually masked the presence of illegal whisky stills from the excise men.

The ancient Egyptians used the juniper's astringent berries in medicine, mainly for digestive problems such as flatulence and to expel tapeworms. Seventeenth-century herbalist Nicholas Culpeper agreed that juniper aided indigestion, also suggesting the juice would make an effective counter-poison to various venoms. By now, too, the tree had acquired another reputation, as an abortifacient. If a woman gave birth "under the savin tree", it was understood she had been artificially induced with a concoction of juniper.

Generally, however, the juniper was considered a tree of protection. Hares were said to hide in it from pursuing hounds, who would lose the scent in the branches, and in Italy junipers were grown by doorways because passing witches would be compelled to stop and count the innumerable leaves. It was considered unlucky to cut one down, and in Germany, people, on passing, removed their hats out of respect for Frau Wachholder, the spirit of the tree. A strange German story sees a wicked stepmother punishing a boy for stealing an apple. She kills him, boils his flesh for soup and hides his bones under a juniper where, many years before, his true mother had been buried. The tree bursts into fire, releasing a bird that broadcasts the story across the land. It then drops a millstone onto the stepmother, re-enters the flames and reappears as the boy.

To dream of juniper if you are already ill foretells that you will not recover, but dreaming of its berries prophesizes success, or the birth of a boy.

Opposite Juniper (*Juniperus communis*) from *Köhler's Medizinal-Pflanzen*, 1887.

The Submerged Forest

"Seaweed" is a general term for several kinds of organisms that live underwater, but not all such "weeds" are plants.

For example, kelp (*Laminariales*) may look like a bizarre grass, with its long straps of undulating "leaves" waving in the currents, but it belongs to an entirely different kingdom – heterokont, a group of organisms that mainly includes algae.

Kelp grows in vast forests, wherever it can find somewhere to anchor itself, using a branched organ called a "holdfast", which looks like roots but cannot absorb or distribute nutrients. Some species have gas-filled floating devices called pneumatocysts to raise the kelp as close as possible to the light for photosynthesis. Many kelp grow at an extraordinary rate, up to half a metre a day. Their density helps to cushion coastlines from the worst of oceanic storms.

Seagrasses, on the other hand, are plants, many of which even flower. There are around 60 species, forming massive underwater meadows, that are home to some of the most diverse ecosystems in the world, providing rich habitats and acting as carbon sinks. It has been suggested that fishermen's tales of mermaids may have come from glimpses of a marine mammal, the dugong, swimming through seagrass beds.

Unsurprisingly, few of our ancestors differentiated much between types of "seaweed" other than to work out which were most useful in the pot or around the home. And useful it is. Different seaweeds (often kelp) can be found in soaps, dyes, glass and even toothpaste. Many forms are highly nutritious. It is good for human food, animal fodder, fishing lines, buttons and, dried, as bedding, and gardeners still prize seaweed as a powerful fertilizer. There is, however, a distinct difference in attitudes to the harvest of the seas, depending on geographical location.

In the West, anyone forced to eat seaweed has usually been considered the poorest of the poor. During the Irish potato famine, peasants hauled seaweed up the shore, either to eat or in a desperate attempt to fertilize their crops. In Aberdeenshire, Scotland, the first harvest of each year was traditionally celebrated by leaving a dollop of stinking – but highly serviceable – seaweed on the doorstep of every croft in the village. When not using it for medicine (it is a valuable source of iodine), people hung dried strands of another seaweed, bladderwrack (*Fucus vesiculosus*), by their doors to act as a natural barometer. Indoors, a bunch of seaweed hung by the fireplace warded off evil spirits.

Opposite Kelp (*Lamenaria*) from *Köhler's Medizinal-Pflanzen*, 1887.

Laminarieae.

Laminaria Cloustoni Edm.

Some of these spirits came from the sea. In Viking culture, the horrific seaweed-haired draugr were originally the undead who had drowned, threatening the living with grasping tentacles. Another Norse demon, the nuckelavee (Devil of the sea) might be repelled by burning seaweed on the shore. For the Celts, mermaids called "merrows" seduced fishermen through tumbling locks of seaweed. A fisherman might steal their magic, usually in the form of a cap or shawl, to make her stay, but it could only ever be temporary: she would always return to the sea.

In ancient Greek mythology, Glaucus the fisherman ate some magical seaweed, was turned part-fish, covered in seaweed and barnacles and had to live in the sea. The upside was that he was granted the gift of prophecy. The Greek goddess

Amphitrite, consort of Poseidon, wears a seaweed crown. She is known as Salacia in Roman mythology. Neptune's queen, complete with a seaweed crown, her name comes from the Latin *sal* and she rules all salt water. Oddly, in botany, *Salacia* is a genus of woody climbing plants that have nothing to do with the ocean.

La Pincoya is a mermaid who dances on the beaches of Chile, covered in kelp. If she faces the sea, fishing will be good. If she faces the mountains, fishermen should stay onshore. In New Mexico, the creator god Awonawilona is said to have fashioned all the other gods from seaweed.

Japanese people love seaweed. The *shōjō* is a sea spirit with bright red hair, seaweed girdle and a fondness for alcohol who can tell the quality of a person's soul. *Minogame* and *hōnengame* are male and female sea turtle spirits with streaming seaweed hair. He represents longevity, she can tell the future. The *Taihō Ritsuryō* law, written in 701 CE, stated that three varieties of seaweed – wakame, arame and nori – could be used instead of money to pay taxes to the imperial court.

Similarly, in Korea new mothers were traditionally given seaweed soup after giving birth. The Haenyeo "women of the sea" are a tough, semi-matriarchal community of freedivers who continue to live on the seaweed they harvest from depths of up to 30 metres.

In China, it was said that *k'uh-lung* (similar to dragons) hatched from eggs of jewelled seaweed.

Opposite Seaweed by Ellen Hutchins, early nineteenth century. Kew Collection.

Above Art by Arthur Rackham, from *Siegfried and the Twilight of the Gods* by Richard Wagner, 1911.

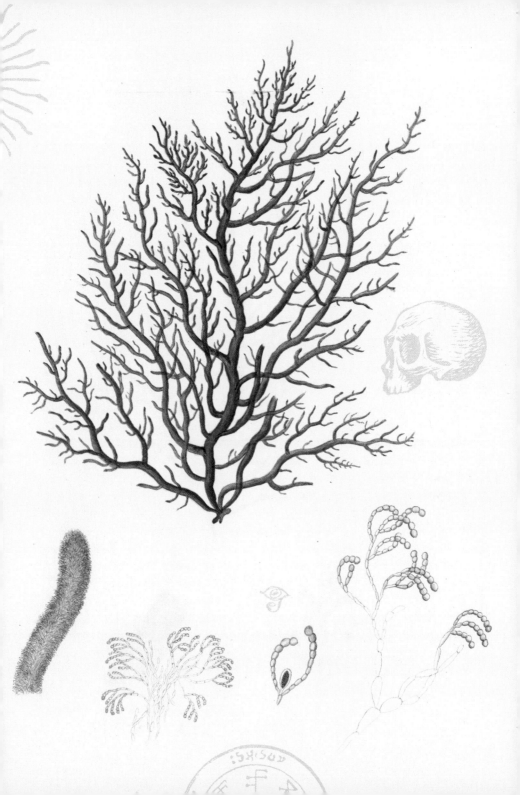

Aspen

Populus tremuloides

In ancient times the "quaking tree" was the tree of heroes. Aspen's quaking leaves (remembered in the Latin name, *tremuloides*), worn as a crown, lent the wearer the power to descend into the Underworld and, more importantly, to return.

It has been suggested that the aspen crowns found in ancient burials were intended as a passage to rebirth.

The tree's common name comes from the ancient Greek aspis, the convex wooden shield wielded by the Spartans. It is unlikely these were made from aspen, since the tree prefers the cooler regions of Europe, Asia and North America. The Celts' aspen shields, however, were not just lightweight and easily carved, they were also believed to carry protective properties to the bearer. Cuchulain, the legendary hero of Ulster, bore such a shield, to purge him of fear.

Aspen's round leaves, on fine stalks, have pale undersides that shiver in the breeze and shimmer in the sunlight. Their rustling sounds like whispers, giving birth to beliefs that the tree was home to talking spirits. A human who was prepared to listen might hear something to their advantage, though they should beware, for it was not unknown for people to be whisked away to Fairyland from under the aspen's boughs. The voices sometimes whispered that the Underworld was near, but this was not necessarily a bad thing; the aspen was known to be an intermediary between worlds. Aspen

wands were buried with Celtic heroes as a symbol of rebirth, and the tree could help the living too. If a fever sufferer pinned a lock of their hair to a branch, chanting: "Aspen tree, Aspen tree, I prithee shake and shiver, instead of me", it was believed the plant would take on the illness in the patient's stead. In Scotland it was a magical tree which, like the Rowan, would afford protection to anyone who grew it by their home, though the luck would be reversed if the tree was felled to build the house.

When Christianity arrived, the fortunes of the aspen itself were reversed as new superstitions arose, and aspen joined the group of trees accused of supplying the wood for Christ's Cross. Good Christians were encouraged to hurl clods, stones and abuse at it and even cut it down.

Aspen is not a big commercial crop, though its lightweight properties are occasionally exploited in boat paddles and surgical splints, and it has been used for floorboards because the wood does not burn well. Its wood is popular with sculptors being easily carved.

Opposite Quaking aspen (*Populus tremuloides*) from *Familiar Trees* by G. E. Simonds Boulger, 1906–7.

Pl.300. Charme commun. Carpinus Betulus L.

Hornbeam

Carpinus betulus

Given the majestic heights and ages that mature hornbeams
can reach, it is perhaps surprising that there exists relatively
little folklore about them.

Literally translating from the Old English for "hard wood", hornbeam is difficult to work. Its close grain blunts tools – not for nothing is it also sometimes known as "ironwood". Once worked, however, it is long-lasting and keeps its shape – useful for the really tough jobs. Gear-pegs in mills and delicate machinery parts, tool handles, piano actions and coach wheels were traditionally made from hornbeam. It is also very pale and smooth, sometimes likened to ivory, making exquisite parquet flooring and detailed chess pieces.

Perhaps the hornbeam's relative obscurity is down to its resemblance to beech (*Fagus*) and indeed it is sometimes known as the "hedge beech". Although both are often found in oak woodland, the two have significant differences. Beech leaves are glossy, with wavy edges, unlike those of the hornbeam which are smaller, and serrated. The two species' catkins may look similar, but in autumn the hornbeam produces clusters of papery seed cases called samaras, more like those of an ash (*Fraxinus*) than the beech's distinctive nuts. In winter the differences are even clearer. In a phenomenon known as marcescence both trees keep their dead leaves, but hornbeam's chocolate brown colouring is little like the beech's coppery-orange hue.

Hornbeam burns long and hot, making it a hugely important firewood. Diarist and dendrophile John Evelyn wrote that it burnt like a candle, and the fuel was even more prized after it had been turned to charcoal. Today the tree is likely to be pleached (interweaved and clipped) into hedges in large formal gardens, but in the past, hornbeam was one of the most important trees of the managed forest. Grown-out "stools" mark ancient coppiced or pollarded woodland. The gnarled trunks of the most ancient specimens, which have been likened by some to Celtic knots, have sometimes been described as ladders between worlds. The tree has been an important species for the wildlife realms since antiquity.

Historically, hornbeam has been useful medically, too. Its bark was boiled for a muscle-soak, its leaves used to stop bleeding and dress wounds. Today it is an important ingredient in the flower remedy system created by Dr Edward Bach in the early twentieth century. What the tree lacks in folklore is easily made up for in folk use.

Opposite Hornbeam (*Carpinus betulus*) from *Flora von Deutschland* by Otto Wilhelm Thomé, 1885.

Chapter 5:
The Enchanted Forest

Just after the last ice age, 57 per cent of the world's habitable land was covered in forest. With no records apart from the odd cave painting or stone carving, we can only imagine the tales told around a Neolithic campfire as the shadows encroached. We have no idea if these were stories of gods or ghosts, demons or monsters or indeed whether our ancestors found the dense woodland surrounding them frightening or comforting.

From fairy stories to anime, the forest plays a huge role in our imaginations. Its role has changed – and at the same time stayed the same – across millennia as legends of heroes, monsters, nymphs and fairies slowly morph into stories about ourselves.

In the ancient Greek world, dryads were nymphs, the spirits of trees and woodlands. Some, called hamadryads, were tied to a specific tree, born as it germinated, and flourished or diminished with the plant's fortunes. Others watched over a species, including Syke, nymph of the fig (*Ficus carica*), Ptelea, who guarded the elm (*Ulmus*), and Morea, dryad of the mulberry, which remembers her in its scientific name *Morus*.

The stories we have told of the enchanted forest ever since could be said to derive from such nymphs, as well as from the many gods and goddesses worshipped in the ancient world: Tapio, Finnish god of the forest; Medeina, Lithuanian goddess of trees and woodlands; Porvata, Polish god of the woods. Scores of nature-related deities across the globe prove just how important the forest and its care was to our ancestors. Māori legends of how the god Tāne hated living in the darkness so much that he led his siblings in a rebellion, forcing apart their parents, the Earth and the sky, ostensibly explain how trees keep the sky from falling in. If the tale is not necessarily believed literally today, Tāne is still an important idea, an example of how leadership, courage and working together can work for good.

The fairy stories that form the enchanted forest of mythology have many similar themes to those ancient tales but they tend to become more structured as they are told over and over again. Twentieth-century folklorists such as Vladimir Propp and Joseph Campbell studied hundreds of folktales from different cultures. They identified recurring

Left The frontpiece of the book *The Enchanted Forest* by William Bowen, illustrated by Maud and Miska Petersham, 1920.

Opposite *Sleeping Beauty*, illustration by Julius Diez of the classic tale, c. 1900.

"archetypes", many of which relate to the idea of the forest as a metaphor for the unknown. An archetype can refer to a type of story – rags to riches, the quest, overcoming the monster, etc. – or to a kind of character that turns up constantly in such stories.

Joseph Campbell famously stated that the hero enters "the forest" – which may or may not be literal – at the darkest point in their quest. There is no path, so they must forge their own, and it is the wisdom derived from the choices they make along the way

that becomes their true reward.

The famous European fairy stories, not least those collected by the Brothers Grimm or reworked by Charles Perrault, often use a literal forest as their setting, leaving readers to enjoy them on whichever level they choose. Villains are usually clear-cut, such as the witch who incarcerates Hansel and Gretel, the evil fairy wishing revenge on Sleeping Beauty or the sorceress that incarcerates Rapunzel. Snow White's evil queen disguises herself as a kindly old woman

and Little Red Riding Hood's wolf masquerades as Granny, but even such villains are hardly difficult to spot. Others are more challenging. Just who is the bad guy in *Beauty and the Beast*, for example? The original fairy tale sees the pride of the merchant's two oldest daughters as the evil that their youngest sister must ultimately challenge. The animated Disney version goes further, laying the villainy with the entire village marching through the woods, torches lit, perhaps representing humanity as the enemy of the forest.

This is not entirely new. A Swiss folk tale tells of a woodcarver from the mountain village of Reckingen who, deep in the forest, hears a magical voice singing the loveliest melody he has ever heard. He brings the rest of his village to hear the little fir tree from which the voice trills so happily. Enchanted by the music, the people visit the fir tree for years just to listen to its joyful music, but eventually the village elders give the by-now obsessed sculptor permission to cut it down. The carver spends the rest of his life making his masterwork: a statue of the Virgin Mary, both beautiful and lifelike. The villagers place the sculpture on the church altar and stand back. The statue begins to sing again, this time a heartbroken lament. At the end the statue falls silent and never sings again.

Modern interpretations of folk tales and new fantasy built on folkloric themes and character types tend to carry clear, often environmental messages about humankind and its relationship to the forest. The 1997 Japanese animation *Princess Mononoke* carries many traditional fairy-tale tropes but brings with it an unmistakable horror of the industrial world. Set in the medieval Muromachi period of Japan, it has recognizable folkloric heroes, mentors, tricksters and gatekeepers, but a dark shadow hangs over the heroes and their setting: human activity. Another mysterious character, the Forest Spirit, is not a classic "good" or "bad" character either. Representing life and death, and based on the Japanese deer god Yatsukamizuomitsuno, it protects the Cedar Forest and, as the fearsome humanoid Night Walker, can destroy as easily as it can heal. The enchanted forest is not a place of comfort.

Opposite *The Babes in the Wood* by Randolph Caldecott, c. 1846.

Lightning Trees

There are few more evocative sights than a lone,
leafless tree on a hill or in a field, its wood jagged and
silver, having been ravaged by a lightning strike.

Such a tree is easily enough explained today as a prime target for atmospheric electricity to find the shortest way to Earth, but before science worked this out, thunderstorms were the work of the gods.

Every religion had a god of thunder. Zeus, Thor, Ba'al, Set, Ukko, Perkūnas, Leigong, Indra, Raijin, Xolotl, Tlaloc, Illapa, Shango, Whaitiri and Mamaragan are just a few of the scores of deities entrusted with the phenomenon, nearly always also the kings of the gods. In several Baltic religions, trees struck by lightning became sacred places, because Perun, god of thunder, now lived there. It was no coincidence that the mighty oak (*Quercus*) was sacred to various gods of thunder but thanks to its height – and high water content – it is also a regular victim to lightning strikes. Ash (*Fraxinus*) has long been considered a "magnet" for lightning, perhaps because it has a tendency to split as it ages, making it look as though it has been struck.

First Nation Cherokee placed great store by lightning trees, believing they had absorbed the lightning's energy. If the tree was still alive, it was even more precious, as the magical properties still coursed through its wood. Edwardian ethnographer James Mooney, who lived with the Cherokee for several years, wrote that the energy could be dangerous. Regular people did not touch or burn it for firewood and believed that throwing it into a field would destroy a crop. Designated medicine men soaked the next year's seeds in water along with mashed lightning-struck greenwood to ensure a good harvest, and burned splinters to charcoal, with which ballplayers painted their faces, so they might "strike their opponents with all the force of a thunderbolt".

The wood from a lightning-struck tree was sometimes thought to work as a charm against being hit, a belief perhaps deriving from the widespread folk belief that it is not possible to be struck twice. Yet the image of the blasted oak is not always a happy one. Wales, in particular, carries stories of horrors residing in lonely, scorched trunks. *The Haunted Oak of Nant Gwrtheyrn*, for example, tells of Rhys, a grief-mad bridegroom who discovers the skeleton of his wife Meinir in the bowels of the lightning tree many years after her disappearance, still wearing her tattered wedding gown. During a game of hide and seek at the wedding, Meinir had hidden in the old oak, the young couple's favourite courting spot, but become entangled in its branches.

Opposite A print of Roman priests exorcizing trees which had been struck by lightning.

Ceubren yr Ellyll.
The Haunted Oak.

Hollow Trees

Hollow trees are the domain of the fairies. They may act
as travellers' shelters, boundary markers and even the
local hanging tree, but they always carry mystery.

Such trees can be the work of the lightning gods; more often they have become hollow from sheer old age. Bracket fungus performs a useful task in the forest, breaking down heartwood within an old tree, ready for small creatures to clear it away. The tree is hollowed from the inside, but new growth is rarely attacked and the host may continue to grow for hundreds of years. The largest become local, even national wonders. Some have arches or doors cut into them and are used as shrines, chapels and even taverns.

The Femeiche is the oldest living tree in Germany. It was once known as the Raven Oak, referring to Odin's sacred bird, implying it was already an impressive specimen in pre-Christian times. A wooden church was built to "convert" the tree, a decent outcome when so many "heathen" trees were hacked down by missionaries. It later became the Justice Oak, under which court judgements were pronounced. In 1750, the dead heartwood was removed and a door fitted. It was visited by Prince Friedrich Wilhelm of Prussia on 26 September 1819, who inspected 36 fully-armed infantry soldiers inside the tree before breakfasting with his generals.

In Greenwich, London, a young Elizabeth I is said to have picnicked around Queen Elizabeth's Oak before, a couple of centuries later, its hollow trunk was turned into the local lock-up. Crowhurst in Surrey boasts a magnificent yew (*Taxus baccata*) that was already a cavern when the Johns Evelyn and Aubrey (respectively diarist and antiquarian) visited. An English Civil War cannonball was found embedded in its trunk in the nineteenth century while it was being converted into a summerhouse.

Hollow trees near healing springs were once used in folk medicine. The sick person had to creep through the hole in the tree, sometimes but not always naked, a specific number of times on a specific day and at a specific time, which varied according to local tradition. This transferred the disease – rickets, epilepsy, boils, gout, or any number of other ailments – to the tree. Christians also recognized the mystical value of a hollow tree. In 1415 peasants from the town of Scherpenheuvel, Belgium placed a statue of the Virgin Mary in an oak cavity, where fever sufferers prayed to it. It was said that a shepherd who tried to steal the statue was paralyzed on the spot until someone returned the icon. Later, in 1603, three separate witnesses saw it drip blood.

Hollow trees may be haunted. A mysterious "White Lady" sits and spins in a hollow tree in Soeren Forest, Netherlands. The *Witte Juffer* will punish a rude intrusion, but reward those who treat her with respect.

Opposite *Ceubren yr Ellyll: The Haunted Oak* by lithographers Day & Haghe, c. 1850.

The Hero in the Forest

Psychologists derive great enjoyment analyzing the
classic theme of the hero stepping into a terrifying forest
of myths, legends and fairy tales. The motif has been
with us since the earliest times, however, as a story-
friendly way of exploring our own demons.

We are hard-wired to be both intrigued by and suspicious of the dark shadows in the brightest wood. Sometimes a hero will leave the safety of the village in search of adventure. Many Arthurian legends begin with a knight setting out from Camelot in search of glory, sometimes just for the sheer fun of the chase. The Questing Beast of medieval literature, for example, apparently haunts its forest for no other reason than to be chased and killed. Other heroes enter the woods with specific goals. Little Red Riding Hood wants to visit her grandmother. The Prince is searching for Rapunzel's tower. Hansel and Gretel have been dragged into the woods and must now find their way home. It is up to each individual to learn which cackling crones, wise old hermits, talking animals and beautiful fairies are enemies in disguise and which may be genuine mentors.

The two great epics of Indian mythology both see their heroes exiled to the forest, shorthand for "religious enlightenment". The *Ramayana* tells of the 14-year retreat of Rama, one of the most popular avatars of the god Vishnu, during his spell as an earthly prince. The *Mahabharata* follows the fortunes of the five Pandava brothers, exiled to the forest with their brave and vengeful wife, Draupadi, after being tricked in a game of dice. Here they find the strength to face their enemies in the second part of the story.

Some heroes live in the forest, including the mage Merlin and the folk hero Robin Hood. Each understands the wood and is able to merge into its shadows. Other woods are actively benevolent. A magic comb given to the heroine of *The Witch*, a Russian fairy tale, turns into an enchanted forest, concealing the girl from the witch Baba Yaga.

It is often suggested that the hero of myth represents each of us as we face challenges in our lives, and that the ways heroes face up to their foes, fight them and survive, give us hope for our own problems. Yet no hero is the same after having passed through the wood. They have been forced to act, showing us that we too, cannot stay passive in the face of poverty, loss or threat.

Opposite A lithograph of Robin Hood from the nineteenth century.

Parasites and Epiphytes

Trees rarely stand alone. Each is its own ecosystem,
supporting life, from insects and animals to other plants.
Some are more welcome than others.

Parasitic plants derive some or all their nutrients from another "host" organism, often a tree. They generally attach themselves via an organ, the haustorium, that penetrates the host's stem or root, and either take only water and minerals (hemiparasites) or all their nutrition (obligates or holoparasites) from the host plant. Many of these plants have strange, almost ghostly properties due to a complete lack of chlorophyll, the green pigment that allows most plants to photosynthesize (make oxygen and energy from the sun).

The common toothwort, *Lathraea squamaria*, is a fine example of a holoparasite. Typically ghostly white, it derives all its nutrients from its host, usually the hazel (*Corylus*), but also elm (*Ulmus*), alder (*Alnus*) and willow (*Salix*). For most of the year it hides below ground. In the spring it shoots out scaly, snake-like flowers, often some distance from the tree, demonstrating how far roots can extend. Oddly, these strange-looking plants have attracted virtually no folklore, though in Yorkshire they are known as corpse-flower and in Hampshire cuckoo-flower.

The scales have been likened to rows of discoloured teeth but there is no evidence that "tooth-wort" was used to cure toothache as might be suggested by the doctrine of signatures. John Gerard's 1597 *Herbal* suggests that, as "clownes

lung wort", it could be useful in treating lung conditions. The common toothwort's more colourful cousin, purple toothwort (*Lathraea clandestina*), is another holoparasite. It loves the damp woodlands and streams of northern Europe, colonizing the roots of poplars (*Populus*) and willows (*Salix*).

Monotropa uniflora, the ghost flower, Indian pipe, corpse plant or American ice plant, has also lost all colour to become a staggeringly lovely, translucent cluster of bell-like flowers. It grows throughout the United States, with the beech (*Fagus*) as its preferred host. A 1917 guidebook, *Wild Flowers Worth Knowing*, reveals the plant's previous reputation as evil, describing its parasitic nature as "the lowest stage of degradation…branded with the mark of crime as surely as was Cain." Cherokee legend tells how the Great Spirit turned the chiefs of several tribes into these eerie, pipe-like plants after they had quarrelled over the peace pipe. Ghost-flower juice was sometimes used as an eye lotion, but later it was used to treat spasms and fainting, giving it the nicknames "convulsion weed" and "fit-root".

Opposite A white Ghost Flower (*Monotropa uniflora*) flowering on the forest floor. This all–white plant without chlorophyll is parasitic on other plants.

Left An illustration of the red rider for the fairytale, *Vasilisa the Beautiful*, 1899.

Opposite The Pandavas go into exile in the forest for 13 years, as seen in the Indian epic *Mahabharata*.

Epiphytes, on the other hand, grow on other plants but derive their moisture and nutrients from the air or local debris. They may take many forms, not least some mosses (Bryophyta) and liverworts (Marchantiophyta) found in virtually any forest in the world. Some – holoepiphytes – spend their entire lives without contact with the ground, others – hemiepiphytes – eventually make contact with the ground. The famous northern rata (*Metrosideros robusta*) of New Zealand begins life growing from seeds dropped by birds onto a host, often the rimu (*Dacrydium cupressinum*). As it grows, it does not actively take nutrients from the tree, but the rata's massive root system slowly encases its support, eventually smothering it to look like a tree itself. [Ivy (*Hedera*), often condemned for similar qualities, is neither parasitic nor epiphytic: it derives its nutrients from the soil, and merely uses specialized hairs on its climbing stems for support.] The plant takes its name from a Māori hero called Rātā, about whom hundreds of tales are told. In one legend he cuts down a tree without first making the proper rituals and is punished by the forest folk. Traditionally the rata tree's knobbly bark was made into lotions or poultices; the nectar from its bright red flowers was used for sore throats.

Not all orchids (Orchidaceae) are epiphytes, but those that are have thick, spongy aerial roots to absorb and store water and nutrients. Bulging pseudobulbs, specializing in water storage, help them to tolerate droughts. The plant's name comes from these, and the Greek word *orkhi*s or "testicle". Orchis, son of a satyr and a nymph (both associated with woodlands and the erotic), was chopped into pieces by Dionysus after attempting to rape a priestess while drunk. His heartbroken father prayed to the gods, and flowers grew where the body parts fell. The first-century physician Dioscorides associated orchids with aspects of reproduction, aphrodisiacs and sex determination. Men who ate orchid roots were thought to father sons; women who wanted daughters were advised to eat the small roots.

The Totonac people of Central America tell a different story, of a princess, Janat, who loved against her father's wishes. The king severed the young man's head in the forest and orchids grew from splashes of his blood. In China, Confucius considered the flower's beauty to represent friendship between superiors.

Orchids – an enormous family – have a wide variety of folk uses, according to species and location. They have been food, religious amulets, perfumes and flavourings – not least from the *Vanilla* genus. In medicine they have been used to cure anything from arthritis and dysentery to sickness in elephants. A famous Turkish dessert, *salepli dondurma*, is made from salep, *Orchis mascula*, a species that forms two very large pendulous tubers. The name literally translates as "fox-testicle ice cream". The same plant is also said to cure skin problems, bronchitis and hunchbacks.

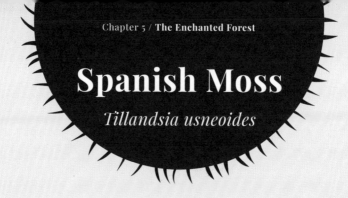

Spanish Moss

Tillandsia usneoides

The evil pirate Gorez Goz was over six feet tall, with a beard black as coal reaching down to his waist. It is told that he captured a Native American Cusabo chief whose daughter offered herself in exchange – if he could catch her.

Gorez Goz chased the girl into the swamp but became lost. He heard a voice above his head, taunting him from the top of a great oak tree. Furious, he climbed after her, but became tangled in the branches, even as she jumped to safety into the creek. The pirate tried to follow, but the tree held him fast. He died there and his beard continues to grow. It may look grey now, but remove its scales and the "moss" inside is still jet black. Other legends of this strange, vegetal drapery involve a Spanish explorer forbidden to marry a local girl and tied to a tree, where he died, and a couple murdered on their wedding day; the moss is the bride's hair.

Spanish settlers called it French hair, French settlers called it Spanish beard; over the years the difference has been split and it is now Spanish moss, but *Tillandsia usneoides* is neither moss nor Spanish. It is an epiphytic plant from the Bromeliaceae family that grows in tropical and subtropical climates. It is most famous in the swamps, creeks and bayous of the south-eastern United States, hanging, silvery, grey-green, from the live oak (*Quercus virginiana*) and bald cypress (*Taxodium distichum*). It is a mystical, mysterious presence throughout the region, tumbling from its host, growing in slender "chains" of curling, needle-like foliage.

The plant is often found in low-lying cemeteries, where the water levels constantly threaten the graves, adding atmosphere to ghost stories. Yet another legend speaks of Alice Riley, the first woman hanged in Georgia, in 1735. Unlike the rest of the city of Savannah's trees, which are covered in Spanish moss, no *Tillandsia usneoides* will grow on any planted in Wright Square, her execution spot. Her ghost still walks there but the plant cannot take where innocent blood has been spilled.

The Houma people of Louisiana treated fever with Spanish moss, and it was also used by enslaved Africans for respiratory problems and diabetes. Modern scientific exploration has suggested that it may help regulate blood glucose levels, but not as food. Spanish moss will not kill you but is unpleasant to eat, not least because of the variety of wildlife – from insects to bats and snakes – that it supports.

Opposite A large old oak tree covered in Spanish moss in Southwest Florida.

XII, 1.   105 Rosaceae. 1 Pruneae.

394. Prunus spinosa L.   Schlehdorn.

Blackthorn

Prunus spinosa

The midnight-blue fruits of the blackthorn, with their
customary powdery "bloom", are too tart for most people's
tastes, but they do present a classic flavouring for gin.

For many years the delightful blossoms of the blackthorn were not allowed indoors, part of a general superstition that white flowers represented death. This is a shame, since the single white flowers, with their "sparkles" of dancing stamens, are some of springtime's prettiest sights.

Blackthorn often blooms during a cold snap after unseasonably warm weather, leading to the idea of a "blackthorn winter", the period before which crops should not be sown. The one exception is barley, which is best planted while the sloe blossom reigns.

Blackthorn is another plant said to have been used in Christ's Crown of Thorns, and it was sometimes thought a blackthorn scratch would give a victim blood poisoning. Generally, however, the blackthorn's many affectionate local names – including buckthorn, scrogg, heg-pegs, snag-bush and winter kecksies – prove it to be a popular plant. In Dorset small sloes are "snegs"; a young blackthorn is a "gribble". The same name is given to a knobbly walking stick made from blackthorn wood.

A wand made from wood borne by the "dark crone of the woods", the "keeper of secrets", was said to protect the wielder from witches' spells, but blackthorn enjoys an uneasy relationship with folklore. Some thought witches used the thorns to prick waxen poppets, while the ghost of Major Thomas Weir, executed for witchcraft in Scotland in 1670, still carries the blackthorn staff that was burned with him. In an Irish story, the hero throws a sloe stone over his shoulder, foiling his pursuers with the impenetrable hedge that magically springs from it. The magical forest surrounding the castle in some versions of *Sleeping Beauty* is blackthorn, though Rapunzel's prince is also sometimes blinded by the plant's thorns.

The mayor of Sandwich, Kent has carried a blackthorn staff since at least the fourteenth century and the famous Black Rod carried by a sergeant at arms in the British House of Lords is a not much younger idea. In Ireland, the traditional *shillelagh*, or fighting club, is also made from blackthorn's dense, gnarled wood.

Blackthorn sloes are too astringent to be eaten, but the juice was prescribed for dysentery by Greek physician Andromachus, a remedy continued by Culpeper in his famous *Herbal*. Neat, it was used as a mouthwash; sweetened as a cordial it soothed colds and coughs. In Somerset, homemade sloe wine was not thought alcoholic. Even teetotallers considered themselves safe drinking the brew. Oh, how we fool ourselves.

Opposite Blackthorn (*Prunus spinosa*) from *Flora von Deutschland* by Otto Wilhelm Thomé, 1885.

Chapter 6:
Cures for
the Body

From *khorisa*, a bamboo paste used in northern India for impotence, to the old Hampshire tradition of drinking from a cup carved of holly wood to cure whooping cough; from an ancient Assyrian apple treatment for venereal disease to the traditional Peruvian anti-malaria drug quinine, the number of tree-related cures is impossible to count. The history of trees within the medical world often collides with spiritual teaching, ancient principles of balance, and even trial-and-error methods of folkloric wisdom.

Trees have probably been used as medicine since humanity
began, but it was the ancient Greek philosopher Theophrastus
who first started looking into them in a systematic way.

Born around 370 BCE, he wrote two treatises on botany, *Enquiry into Plants* and *On the Causes of Plants.*

Centuries later, Greek physician Dioscorides wrote about a system of medicine known as the "doctrine of signatures". Plants were used to treat parts of the body or diseases that they resembled, or according to the conditions under which they grew. For example, Dioscorides prescribed the caterpillar plant (*Scorpiurus muricatus*) against scorpion bites because its leaves looked like a scorpion's tail. Sliced open, pomegranates looked a bit like a human jaw and teeth, making them ideal for curing toothache. Willow (*Salix*) thrives in damp conditions, and people with rheumatic problems suffer most when their surroundings are also cold and damp, so willow bark was an obvious prescription. In this particular case, the physicians were on to something. Willow's inner bark contains salicylic acid, the base of our modern-day drug aspirin.

Another popular theory, probably developed by the classical physician Hippocrates, proposed that the body was made up of four "humours", representing the four seasons. These needed to be kept in perfect balance for ideal health. Disease occurred when someone suffered from a surfeit – or paucity – of blood (spring), yellow bile (summer), black bile (autumn) or phlegm (winter). Plants were divided up into the four classes and prescribed to redress any imbalances.

In traditional Indian Ayurvedic medicine, the body depends on three *dosa* or "faults" running in parallel with three *guna* ("virtues"), all of which must align for good health. The balance of two opposing energies, yin and yang, underlies the concepts behind traditional Chinese medicine (TCM). TCM promotes tree-derived medicines but also a more spiritual use of the forest for wellbeing, suggesting that it can absorb carbon, promote biodiversity and, on an individual level, boost physical and mental health merely by humans walking in it. Today, this is a suggestion few would argue with, but treating the whole body has not always been so universally accepted.

In the West, the tendency was to focus on specific conditions, and old habits died hard. It took a long while, for example, for Europeans to catch on to quinine, an anti-malarial drug derived from the Andean fever tree *Cinchona officinalis* by the South American Quechua people in the early seventeenth century. Only in the nineteenth century did it become normal to mix it with sugar and lemon to create "tonic" water, to be drunk with gin.

By the sixteenth and seventeenth century herbalists were creating manuals for general use, listing plants and their uses. English herbalist Nicholas Culpeper had, controversially, made an

Right An old woman collecting herbs by a woodland spring, 19th century.

English translation of *Pharmacopoeia Londinensis*, an apothecary's textbook which the Royal College of Physicians had conspired to keep secret from ordinary folk. Culpeper was determined that even poor people should be able to afford medicines, and suggested hedgerow alternatives for expensive potions. His *Complete Herbal* took this a step further, specifically describing the uses of wild plants using the doctrine of signatures, concepts of the humours and astrology. It is still in print today.

Culpeper's use of the water found within a beech hollow is a good example of another way folklore has used trees for their "presence" as much as for their bark, roots, leaves or fruit. In some traditions, trees can bear the weight of a human's illness for them. In Hampshire, England, a sick child would be passed through an ash (*Fraxinus*) that had been split down the trunk. The tree was then tightly bound. The child was believed to regain its health as the tree healed.

We are still discovering the therapeutic qualities of trees. The ancient yew (*Taxus*), for example, has been of limited medicinal use, thanks to its well-known poisonous qualities, yet recent research has reassessed those toxins and the chemotherapy drug docetaxel is now used to treat lung, prostate and breast cancers. Medicine is not done with trees yet.

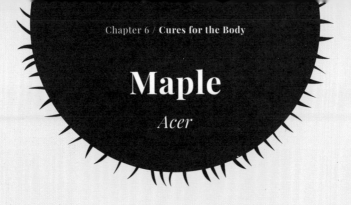

Maple

Acer

While maples may be found across the world, two powerful images pervade the many-branched *Acer* family: the graceful, many-coloured Japanese symbol of Autumn, and the North American fountain of wintertime sweetness.

According to a tale that the Saulteaux tell, Nanaboozhoo, the trickster god of many First Nations people, was grateful to the multicoloured sugar maple (*Acer saccharum*) for shielding his grandmother from evil Little People. He caused the tree to make sweet sap, and taught humans how to tap it using birch bark containers known as *mokuks*. Other legends say it was discovered by a woman with moose meat to cook, who tapped the trees to find water. She left it to boil but on returning found the moose cooked to nothing but a sticky mess. She hid from her husband in shame, but on creeping back found him feasting upon it. A Chippewa story tells of how a wicked magician was turned into a sugar maple tree after the hero Mishosha reversed his spells and conquered the animals of the forest.

Maple sugar is so revered in Canada that the leaf forms part of the national flag; it is equally loved in New England in the US. "Sugaring" has its own traditions and customs. First Nations people often condensed the sap into solid sugar, which was easier to transport than syrup. Later, settlers brought iron and copper kettles. The season – known as the Sugar Moon – runs from midwinter through to springtime,

any time that the sap is not frozen in the trees. When the frogs begin to sing, sugar sappers know it is time to take the "frog run", their last batch. As it is turned to syrup, many sugar-makers still celebrate with a Sugaring Off party. The four grades of syrup, from dark to light amber, do not denote quality, but indicate what uses they are best for. One of the most popular dishes is Sugar-on-Snow, where hot, caramelized syrup is poured in ribbons on to a ball of packed snow and served with sour pickles and doughnuts.

The Japanese maple (*Acer palmatum*) is known as *kito*, meaning peace, or calm, for the serenity of its leaves. As it turns, however, its fiery hues make *momijigari*, or "leaf-hunting" parties, a time for wearing kimonos with maple leaf designs (they are the autumn equivalent to the springtime *hanami*, "blossom viewing"). The custom is said to have begun in the eighth century Heian period, when aristocratic banquets celebrated the leaves with classical *waka* poetry. Maple is a common tree used for the bonsai art of miniaturization, but in Osaka, the leaves are fried to make a popular snack.

Opposite Black sugar maple (*Acer saccharum* subsp. *nigrum*) from *The North American Sylva* by François André Michaux, 1819.

Pl. 43.

H. J. Redouté pinx.   Joly sculp.

Black Sugar Maple.
Acer nigrum.

Juglandeae.

Juglans regia L.

Walnut

Juglans

Known by the ancient Greeks as *Karya Basilica* or "royal walnut", these magnificent trees are believed to have originated in Persia and were spread across Central Asia, China and Europe by Silk Road merchants and the armies of Rome and Alexander the Great.

The ancient Greeks believed the walnut represented wisdom and was ruled by Zeus, king of the gods. In Roman mythology he is Jupiter, hence the modern scientific name *Juglans regia*, "royal walnut".

Dionysus, the god of wine, fell in love with Carya, princess of Laconia, and turned her into a walnut tree. Artemis informed the king and queen, who built the goddess a temple in memory of their daughter. Its pillars were carved from walnut wood in the form of female statues called caryatids. The pecan nut, a relative of the walnut, is called *Carya illinoinensis*.

Despite being introduced to Europe millennia ago, the walnut is still considered an exotic import. Its Old English name, *wealhhnutu*, translates as "foreign nut".

Black walnut is considered a "masculine" tree, ruled by fire, and Nicholas Culpeper pronounced it a plant of the sun. Because the fruit resembles a human brain, the doctrine of signatures associates it with headaches, but it has a long list of medicinal uses, including skin conditions such as eczema. The astringent leaves and bark have been prescribed as laxatives, throat gargles and purgatives.

For all its beauty, the walnut is a tree of melancholy.

Some say that those walking beneath its branches will hear the Devil's servants squabbling overhead, and a falling tree portends ill news. It is also said that no crop can grow around it. Indeed, the tree emits the toxic compound juglone, which kills competing vegetation.

Many traditions believe that beating a walnut tree will make it fruit more plentifully. Walnuts are eaten, used for oil, strewed at weddings to symbolize fecundity, used as tools for divination, and even carried in pockets to repel thunderbolts. Husks make inks and dyes. In France, nuts from the "noix de Périgord" make the famous aperitif *quinquinoix* and the walnut wine *vin de noyer*. Even the shells have uses, crushed for industrial processes and skin exfoliants. People of the American First Nations have used the wood for talking sticks and flutes. Several south-eastern tribes talk of a strange figure, the Walnut Cracker, who continued to crack nuts after his death, the sound of which scared sick people back to health.

Walnut trees should never be felled, but dug up, as the best wood is at the base, prized for its use in fine furniture and Jaguar car dashboards.

Opposite Walnut (*Juglans regia*) from *Köhler's Medizinal-Pflanzen*, 1887.

Mango

Mangifera indica

Thought to have originated in the foothills of the Himalayas and spread by humanity as far as China, East Africa and the Philippines, the mango has acquired a saucy reputation as the fruit of unbridled lust.

While the mango's sweet, luscious flesh is a favourite foodstuff, its unctuous juices and heady perfume carry connotations of luxury and exoticism that have not always been positive. In the late twentieth and early twenty-first century, the fruit as a metaphor for all things "exotic" has led to the pejorative description "sari-and-mango" for a novel filled with clichés of tigers, spices and ring-necked parakeets; many feel that this does not represent modern India and Pakistan. The mango has been derided as representing pent-up passion, but these works are only continuing millennia-old traditions. The fourth-century poet Kalidasa, for example, often wrote of the mango blossom in plays and verse, where its fragrance aroused passion in both humans and gods.

In Hindu legend, Kamadeva, the god of love, shot flower-tipped arrows of varying degrees of love. The mango, strongest of all, provoked lust. It is also the fruit of knowledge, after the sage Narada offered a mango to whichever of Shiva and Parvati's two sons could first encircle the world. Instantly, one, Kartikeya, mounted his peacock and disappeared, but the other, Ganesh, announced that his two parents were "the world" to him, walked round them and won the fruit.

The mango is sacred to Shiva. One story, about Karaikal Ammaiyar, the earliest devotional poet of Tamil literature, tells of how her husband sent home two mangoes for his lunch. Before he arrived, however, a devotee of Shiva knocked on the door and the poet gave him one of the fruits. Afraid of what her husband would say, she then prayed to Shiva, who replaced it with an exceptional mango. Her husband did not believe this superb fruit came from the market, so she prayed again and another exquisite mango appeared. The husband fell at her feet in wonder, but now she was unable to concentrate, so she asked the god for one last miracle: to be transformed into an ugly old crone so she could write her poetry in peace.

One of the oddest stories about the mango took place just some 50 years ago, in China, when Chairman Mao regifted a basket of mangoes to some workers who had put down a student rebellion. Not knowing what to do with the strange fruit, the workers caressed and admired them in awe, later placing wax replicas on altars and bowing to them as they passed.

Opposite Mango (*Mangifera indica*) from *Fleurs, Fruits et Feuillages Choisis de la Flore et de la Pomone de L'Île de Java* by Berthe Hoola van Nooten, 1863.

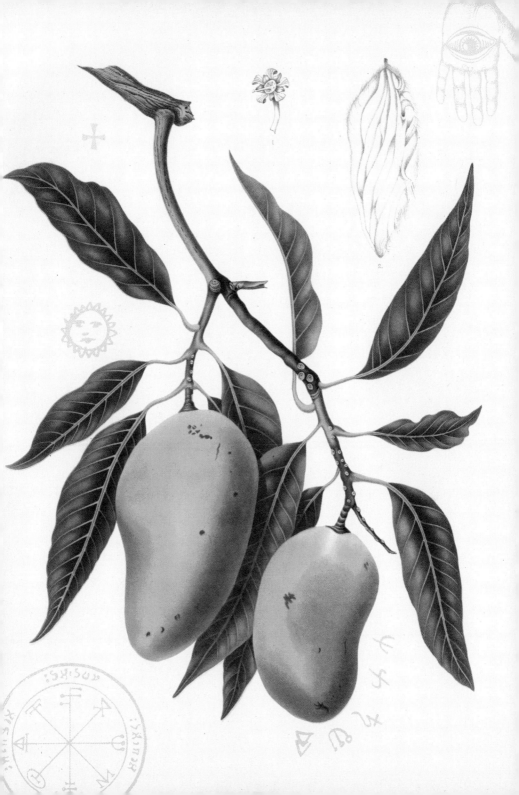

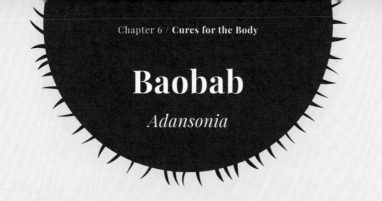

Baobab

Adansonia

Ancient, peculiar, "upside-down" trees, baobabs look for all the world as though they have been uprooted and thrust, headfirst, back into the west-African savanna.

Folklore has many explanations for this. Some claim the Cagn god Thora threw the baobab out of paradise and it continued to grow where it landed. Others say God planted it upside down to stop it walking around, while yet more tales tell how God stuffed it into the ground headfirst because it kept moaning that he'd made it ugly. The baobab has been silently repenting its complaints ever since, by making itself useful.

And useful this great tree is. Reaching 22 metres in height and 25 metres in girth, it can live up to several thousand years, thanks to its extraordinary water-storing capacities. Its seed pods are like skinny melons, full of vitamins and minerals. For those who use it, the baobab can make glue, soap and rubber. In African traditional medicine the fruit treats diseases including fevers, dysentery, smallpox and measles, and is also used as a painkiller. Its timber makes storage, its bark is made into fishnets and clothing. Increasingly, in some countries, entire forests are burned for fuel, making it one of the world's most endangered trees.

Such uses are anathema to many communities, which consider the baobab sacred, not to be touched. The tree is rarely cut in Senegal, and if cuts have to be made, special incantations are said,

begging forgiveness. The Dogon people of Mali forbid the cutting, buying or selling of the Tree of Life. The fourteenth-century emperor Sundiata Keita, according to the *griots* (traditional bards), uprooted an entire baobab, thus awakening the Lion of the Mali Empire. In the past, the most respected *griots* were entombed in baobab trunks after their deaths, to preserve their knowledge. The hollows have also been used as shelters from the sun and, in Nigeria, even prisons.

The creamy-white flowers of the baobab bloom by night. Bush-folk believe spirits live within them; anyone who gathers them will be torn apart by lions. Water in which the seeds have soaked, however, will protect any drinker from crocodiles.

In Madagascar the famous Baobab Amoureux are said to be lovers from separate villages who defied the partners chosen for them by their parents and were turned out of their homes. The couple prayed for help from the gods, who turned them to trees, now twisted together in eternal embrace.

Opposite *African Baobab Tree in the Princess's Garden at Tanjore, India*, by Marianne North, Kew Collection, 1878.

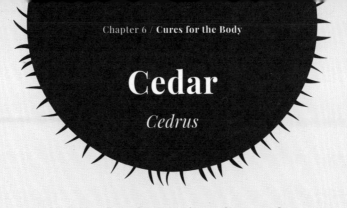

Cedar

Cedrus

The idea of "cedar" changes, depending on where you
are in the world, making folklore even more
complicated than usual.

True cedars, *Cedrus*, belong to the pine or Pinaceae family. The Japanese cedar (*Cryptomeria japonica*) has recently been moved to the Taxodiaceae family. When North American people refer to cedars, they usually mean "false cedars" which may belong to a number of different families, including cypress (*Cupressus*) and juniper (*Juniperus*).

The most famous true cedar, the graceful cedar of Lebanon (*Cedrus libani*), is native to the Middle East and a stalwart of many an English stately home. It appears in the ancient Mesopotamian poem the *Epic of Gilgamesh* where the hero enters a sacred cedar forest guarded by the giant Humbaba. After a great battle, the giant pleads for his life, but Gilgamesh cuts off his head and fells his trees for timber.

The ancient Egyptians revered cedar wood, often beyond precious stones, using it sparingly in sculpture and mummy cases. Its oil was used in the embalming process as an antibacterial fungicide. Today many people still use balls made from cedar wood to deter moths.

"True cedar", "the glory of Lebanon", is mentioned numerous times in the Old Testament. King Solomon built Jerusalem from cedar, including his famous temple, and the tree became associated with purity, protection and eternal life. Jewish people would burn cedar to celebrate a new year, burning away the troubles of the old. Christians carved saints from this most auspicious wood.

It is unclear which "cedar" a Chinese legend refers to where an evil king sets his sights on a married woman and imprisons her husband. When the man dies of grief, the woman throws herself from a cliff. The pair are given separate graves, but a cedar grows from each. The two trunks intertwine into a single tree, known ever since as the Tree of Faithful Love.

Of the many "false cedars", the most famous is the western red cedar (*Thuja plicata*) used by coastal Native Indians of the Pacific for totem poles. For Cherokee and Salish people, cedar wood is imbued with protective spirits. Some carry small pieces in bags around their necks. The wood also made wigwams, canoes, baskets and fishing gear, while the twigs fed fires to tell stories around.

Opposite Cedar of Lebanon (*Cedrus libani*) from *Plantae Selectae* by C. J. Trew and G. D. Ehret, 1760.

Tab. LX.

Cupuliferae.

Fagus silvatica L.

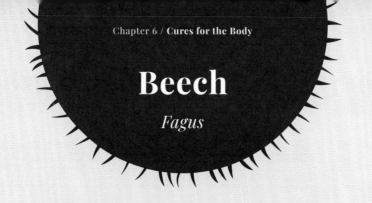

Beech

Fagus

If oak is the King of British trees, it is said that beech is the queen, the Mother of the Woods. Since antiquity, she has guarded over the people who relied on her seeds in times of starvation, and carried pieces of her bark as good luck charms.

The Latin name is directly taken from a minor Gallo-Roman god, Fagus, who ruled over babies and red-headed people, deity to all beech trees, not just the copper-leaved variety (*Fagus sylvatica*). The tree is found in most parts of Europe, from south-east Sweden down as far as northern Sicily.

A beech wood is a place of darkness and mystery. Not even dappled light penetrates its dense canopy. Since its roots also form a dense serpentine "mat" near the surface and its leaves lay a carpet above that, very few other plants attempt to live on a beech forest floor. Small animals, however, enjoy its riches, from caterpillars, who eat the foliage, through to mice, voles, squirrels and birds, who gobble up the seeds. It is also a favourite for truffle-hunters, who know the summer truffle fungus (*Tuber aestivum*) has an ectomycorrhizal arrangement with the beech, exchanging nutrients in return for photosynthesized sugars.

The Argo of Greek mythology may have been built from beech (except for its famous "speaking" prow). Bacchus, god of wine, drank from beech bowls. Henwen, the Welsh "white goddess" who took the form of a sow, is said to have derived her wisdom from eating beechnuts. But humans used it for a different kind of knowledge: the Anglo-Saxon word for beech was *bok*, dating back to a time before paper reached Britain when people wrote on thin slices of beech, eventually making "books".

In the mid-eighteenth century Polin, chief of the Sokokis First Nations people of Sebago Lake, Maine, asked for a dam built by European colonizers to be removed, so his people could continue salmon fishing. Refusal led to a long and bloody war, in which the Sokokis were wiped out. Polin was killed in the Battle of Sebago Lake in 1746. The story of how his body was brought back by canoe is told in *The Funeral Tree of the Sokokis*, by John Greenleaf Whittier. One of Polin's arms was severed, to be buried in consecrated ground, but his brothers bent back a beech sapling enough to place the rest of his body among the roots. The sapling grew into a fine tree, the living embodiment of a lost tribe.

In the West Country of England, strange wrinkled marks on beech tree trunks where the old growth stops were once thought to represent the evil eye.

Opposite Beech (*Fagus sylvatica*) from *Köhler's Medizinal-Pflanzen*, 1887.

The Pine Forest

While for many the pine forest manifests as
the dark, forbidding world of northern European folk
tale, for others pine trees may be seen as anything from
a dense wildwood to a single,
wind-ravaged specimen.

Conifers, a large group of cone-bearing plants known as Pinophyta, comprise several species, including cypresses (*Cupressus*), larches (*Larix*) and redwoods (*Sequoia and Sequoiadendron*), as well as the more familiar firs (*Abies*) and spruces (*Picea*). The different species are often referred to interchangeably in folklore, but most stories surround the pine.

There are more than 100 species of *Pinus*, growing across a range of habitats. The ancient Assyrians were not alone in associating the pine – and especially its cones – with everlasting life. It is a common theme in folklore, perhaps because so many grow to a great age. Indeed, Methuselah, a 4,000-year-old bristlecone (*Pinus longaeva*), is thought to be the oldest living organism on Earth.

In Roman myth the nymph Pitys was pursued by Boreas, the north wind. When he blew her over a cliff, Gaia the Earth Mother took pity on her and turned her clinging form into a pine tree. The hills of Rome are still clothed with *Pinus pinea*, sometimes called umbrella pines for their long trunks and high canopies.

A legend of the Micmac First Nations people tells of three brothers who heard that the mighty magician Glooskap would grant the wishes of any warrior who could find his enchanted lodge. After following a long trail, which included serpents and the Wall of Death, Glooskap granted their wishes. He called on Cuhkw the Earthquake to shake, planting the brothers' feet in the ground and turning them into pine trees, each with the quality he had asked for. The first brother became the tallest tree, the second had the deepest roots, but the third, who had asked for long life, still stands in the forest.

The traditional Japanese *Noh* play *Hagoromo* echoes mermaid tales of northern Europe, where fishermen steal mermaids' clothes, forcing them to stay on land. The fisherman Hakuryo discovers a feathered robe hanging on the branch of a pine tree. A celestial maiden appears, pleading with him to return her hagoromo as she cannot return to heaven without it. He demands something in return, so she dances for him. As soon as she regains her veil, the maiden disappears for ever.

Another tale tells of how a kindly old couple's dog, scratching the earth, discovers gold. A jealous neighbour borrows the dog, but it only uncovers faeces, so he kills it and buries it under a pine tree. The spirit of the dog enters the pine and continues to protect his humans, dropping a branch, which the couple shape into a mortar that magically produces ground barley. The neighbour borrows the mortar, but it only grinds mould and so he burns it. The elderly couple gather the ashes, which restore the pine tree and they are rewarded by the emperor. The neighbour throws ashes at the tree but they fly into the eyes of a passing prince, who has the man whipped.

In yet another Japanese tale, a young couple cannot bear the good-natured village gossip about them, so escape to the forest where they turn into two intertwined pine saplings. Iratsume and Iratsuko still do not want to be disturbed, whispering in the wind, "Do not look at me" and "Do not touch me".

Finland's pines make poignant *merkkipuu*, or "mark trees". A portion of bark is removed and the name, birth and death dates of a deceased loved one carved into the tree's trunk in place of a gravestone. In Scotland, Highlanders split the roots of Scots pine (*Pinus sylvestris*) to use as tapers for their houses and burned pine candles at weddings to bring good luck to the happy couple. Scots pines are said to mark ancient crossroads, boundaries, and the graves of warriors or chieftains. Some say that a particularly grizzled example at Aberfoyle, known as the Fairy Tree, has trapped the spirit of a Reverend Robert Kirk, who tried to understand the language of the fairies and was snatched by the elves in 1692. The tree is covered with clooties (rags) in the hope that it (or perhaps the reverend inside) will grant wishes.

The pineal gland in the human brain, shaped like a pinecone, and which regulates the body's sleep patterns, is known as the "third eye" because it detects light sources. It is perhaps coincidental that Osiris, ancient Egyptian god of the afterlife, is often depicted with a staff of intertwined serpents topped by a pinecone, representing the all-seeing

third eye. Other gods, including the Roman Dionysus and Chicomecōātl the Aztec goddess of agriculture, also wield pinecones, and even within Christianity, the Pope's staff features a pinecone.

Pine is nearly always a symbol of good luck, fertility and longevity, but it is not always so popular. While Guernsey has its own pine forest at Le Guet, to grow such a tree in the garden is said by some to cause the house to be lost; they also warn that anyone falling asleep under a pine will come to an unfortunate end.

Above Stone pine (*Pinus pinea*) from *Herbarium Blackwellianum* by E. Blackwell, 1760.

Linden

Tilia

Filled with shame at giving birth to a monster, the nymph
Philyra begged the gods to turn her into anything that was not
animal. Zeus took pity on the young goddess and changed her
into a linden tree.

Philyra should have waited; her hated son turned out to be Chiron, wisest of all the centaurs, skilled in music, archery, medicinal herbs and science, and mentor to heroes including Achilles, Jason and Heracles.

Tilia is a species known throughout the temperate northern hemisphere, known mainly as linden in Europe, and basswood in North America. Only in Britain is it known as "lime", a confusing term since it is unrelated to any of the Citrus family.

Linden is particularly revered in northern and eastern Europe, but it does not always bring good luck. In Baltic mythology it is sacred to Laima, goddess of fate, who took the form of a cuckoo to pronounce irrevocable prophecies. In Germany, dragons often sleep beneath it, giving them the nickname *lindenworms*. After killing the dragon Fafnir, the hero Sigurd bathed in its blood to gain invincibility. A linden leaf fell on his shoulder, preventing a complete coating and allowing a gap for his enemy Hagen's spear. The linden was blamed.

Despite this hiccup, the linden was a just tree. It was said you could not tell a lie in its shadow, so magistrates sat under the "tree of judgement" to pronounce sentence. *Tilia*'s heart-shaped leaves whispered of love, making the tree sacred to both the Roman Venus and Norse Freya, goddesses of love. During the sixteenth and seventeenth centuries, *tanzlinde* were literally "dancing limes" where celebrations took place. The famous Stufenlinde ("step lime") of Grettstadt is still pruned in "storeys" like a wedding cake. On May Day the town's youth used to dance underneath the decorated tree, inside an octagon of wooden pillars, while the village band played on a platform above them.

The linden has another musical connection in that its wood is said to have excellent acoustic properties and is used for instruments ranging from recorders and percussion instruments to electric guitars. Linden does not warp and can be sanded to a smooth sheen. Indeed, the name comes from the Saxon word *lind* for both "smooth" and "shield". In Switzerland and France, the linden symbolized liberty, and was planted to commemorate great battles. Elsewhere, it was prized by sculptors such as Grinling Gibbons (1648–1721) and, more prosaically, coppiced to make fence posts and rope.

Opposite Linden, basswood or lime tree (*Tilia × europaea*) from *Types de Chaque Famille et des Principaux Genres des Plantes Croissant Spontanément en France* by François Plée, 1844–64.

A

F. Plée pinx.

Chapter 7:
The Sacred Grove

Of all the great sacred groves, perhaps none is more poignant than that of the Druids, sages of the ancient Celtic peoples, described with puzzled respect by Julius Caesar and with curiosity by Roman author Pliny the Elder, for whom the Druids' relationship with the natural world, and especially trees, clearly led to powerful magic. The Romans could not figure out whether to be deeply suspicious of such sorcery, or to learn from it.

The Druid Grove

While Governor of the province of Gaul, Caesar wrote
of the Druids and their veneration of the mighty oak
(*Quercus*). The very word "druid" may come from the
Celtic for "wisdom of the oak".

Those first Druids certainly met and worshipped within *nemetonae*, or sacred groves, but left no written information about themselves. When interest revived in the eighteenth century the Ancient Order of Druids, founded in 1781, had to be reimagined from scratch and was, at first, almost exclusively male. The reinvention continued through the nineteenth century. Sir James Frazer's *The Golden Bough*, published in 1890, solidified some disparate ideas but was not necessarily any more authoritative than earlier works. Modern Druidry is a blend of philosophies, open to all and usually kept private to individuals or orders, with no set belief system or dogma, save that of reverence for nature. Nearly all Druids share a love of the wild and especially of trees, seeing them as beings in their own right. Communing with forests, protecting them, holding ceremonies and meditating within them, or simply being with trees is vital within Druidry, to each in their own way. Bards sing and make poetry. Ovates specialize in divination and healing. Druids are the philosophers and teachers. Many make use of the ogham, or Celtic Tree Alphabet, the encoded wisdom of the trees.

Ogham (literally "language") is probably derived from ancient Irish and consists of various strokes forking from a single stem, not unlike the branches of a tree. It is unclear just how far it dates back; many believe that the earliest of around 400 surviving inscriptions in Ireland and Great Britain are from the fifth to the sixth century CE. Each symbol relates to a tree or shrub: for example, "B" is beithe or birch (*Betula*), "C" is coll or hazel (*Corylus*). In the fourteenth-century Welsh poem, *Cad Goddeu* ("The Battle of the Trees") the hero, Gwydion, enchants a forest full of trees into an animated army. Robert Graves noted that the trees listed in the poem correspond to ogham, allowing scholars to identify any missing parts of the text.

While the Romans wrote of ancient Druids worshipping in oak groves, today's Druids actively support tree-planting schemes specifically focusing on endangered native trees, ascribing different healing and spiritual properties to each species. The sacred grove remains not just a romantic or historical idea, but a powerful, living entity, both spiritually and physically.

Opposite Druids in the Sacred Grove, an illustration from *The Illustrated History of the World*, Ward Lock & Co, 1881.

Opposite The Celtic druid oak and mistletoe ritual as depicted by Henri-Paul Motte, 1900.

Above *Seven Sages in the Bamboo Grove*, Yashima Gakutei, 19th century.

Capuliferae

Quercus pedunculata Ehrh

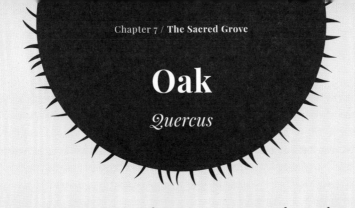

Oak

Quercus

More than 500 species of *Quercus* grow across the northern
hemisphere. It is invariably considered the king of forest trees,
heady with magic and mystery.

The oak is a tree of wisdom in most cultures, sacred to the chief gods in a pantheon, whether Greek, Roman, Norse or Slav. It is no coincidence that the same gods also controlled thunder and lightning, as oak is usually the first tree to be struck. Zeus, king of the Greek gods, fired arrows of lightning at oaks to warn humans of storms, and farmers still sometimes plant the trees as lightning rods.

Oaks growing at the sites of ancient Greek oracles were thought to possess the power of speech, even after being felled. The hero Jason built the prow of his ship *Argo* from an oak growing at the oldest oracle, Dodona, which acted as an advisor on his voyages. In nineteenth-century Britain an oak tree in Derbyshire was said to bleed if a branch was lopped, and screamed prophesies of doom. It was not alone. Everyone knew that, while alive, any oak wielded a protective energy, but that disrespect would be long remembered by this most ancient of trees. A felled oak would wreak revenge in the fullness of time, usually in grisly fashion. At any moment, the culprit might lose an eye, fall lame or drop dead beneath a coincidentally falling branch. Before that, they would be struck with fear whenever they passed an oak forest.

The oak repaid respect, however, with power. The wizard Merlin worked his magic beneath an oak. The legendary hero Robin Hood famously hid his merry men in the shadows of Sherwood Forest when the now-ancient Major Oak was a mere sapling. More convincingly, the fugitive Prince Charles scrambled into an oak at Boscobel House after the Battle of Worcester in 1651, as commemorated by numerous "Royal Oak" pubs around Britain. On 29 May 1660, as King Charles II, he made a triumphant return to London. The date became Oak Apple Day, when people wore sprigs of oak or, better, an oak "apple", a spherical swelling made by the tree around the larvae of the gall wasp. Anyone not wearing such adornment could be pelted with eggs, stung with nettles or pinched, hence the alternative name "Pinch-bum Day".

It is worth inspecting an oak apple on Michaelmas (29 September), as it can tell you what next year's weather will be like. Find a little worm, the year will be pleasant. A spider foretells a barren year, while a fly predicts a moderate season. An empty gall portents death and disease.

Opposite European oak (*Quercus robur* subsp. *robur*) from *Köhler's Medizinal-Pflanzen*, 1887.

Oaks can carry even more sombre connotations. One legend tells that when they learned of Christ's fate, the trees of the forest agreed that none would yield their wood for the execution. The holm oak (*Quercus ilex*) was last to agree, so was cursed to be felled for the cross. Jesus forgave it arguing that it was content to die with him, but holm oak became a "funeral tree" from which ravens squawked ominous tidings. Oak was a hanging-tree in Scotland. It is said that after the execution of Lady Jane Grey the oaks at her home at Bradgate Park, Leicestershire, were "beheaded" in mourning.

The Roman writer Pliny noted the oak was particularly sacred to Druids and the tree has always had an uncomfortable relationship with Christianity. On the one hand, it was dedicated to the Virgin Mary, and in England, "Gospel Oaks" marked stopping places in the annual "beating of the bounds" ceremonies celebrated on Rogation Sunday, when parish boundaries were re-marked with oak rods. Yet the tree also had an ambivalent reputation as a "fairy tree". One of the many accusations faced by Joan of Arc was that instead of going to Mass, she had danced around the Fairy Oak of Bourlémont, adorning it with garlands.

Ordinary people, however, quite liked the idea of a fairy tree. They might touch a "fairy door" (the swelling around the wound where a branch had fallen) to cure diseases, though the charm might not work if nearby church bells had already driven away the Gentle Folk. In Lithuania, folk memories of forest worship saw offerings placed at the roots of oaks. In Vienna, apprentices hammered nails into the trunk of the famous Stock am Eisen "nail tree" before embarking on their compulsory year of wandering. The original Yule log, burned over the 12 days of Christmas, would have been oak and may have had pagan origins. Generally, regular people were pragmatic. During the French Revolution Le Chêne Chapelle, a hollow oak at Allouville near Rouen that had been turned into a chapel in 1696, was saved from the mob when the local schoolmaster nailed a hastily scrawled notice outside, announcing it to be the "Temple of Reason".

A single oak may support around 200 species of organisms, from birds and mammals, through insects and parasitic plants to fungi and algae. Oak has supported humans too since antiquity, providing wood for ships, beams, barrels and furniture, bark for tanning and dyeing and, in times of hardship, acorns for food. Every part of it has, at some point, been used in medicine, especially the bark, which is astringent, useful for treating fevers, diarrhoea and dysentery.

Opposite Gall oak (*Quercus lusitanica*) from *Köhler's Medizinal-Pflanzen*, 1887.

Quercus lusitanica Webb,
var. α infectoria Alph. DC.

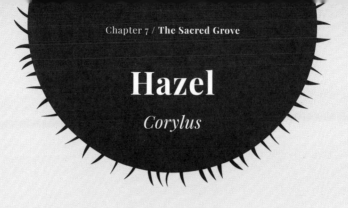

Hazel

Corylus

Its common name might derive from the Anglo-Saxon name for the "little cap" or "haesel" of leaves it wears, but there is nothing cute about the hazel.

Hazel is sacred to the Norse god Thor, the Roman god Mercury, and his Greek equivalent Hermes. For Christians the nuts are the symbol of St Philibert, but in folklore the nuts are guarded by various spirits: in Scotland, the fairy Hind Etin; in the north of England the task falls to Melsh Dick and Churn-milk Peg.

Holy Cross Day, 14 September, was a school nutting holiday, but for older youths, "going nutting" was a euphemism. A girl who "went nutting" on a Sunday would, it was said, meet the Devil and have a baby before she could wed. Gathered nuts were left to mature until Nut Crack night (Halloween) when they were used for divination games. The following day the pastor had to put up with people cracking and eating nuts very noisily in church.

Pilgrims and warriors carried hazel staffs; shepherds bent the young shoots into crooks as they grew. Bringing catkins into the house, however, was thought to impair lambing. Hazel makes water-dowsing rods, while a wand cut on the Sabbath will ward off witches. In parts of Wales, corpses were buried with hazel for the same reason. In Ireland St Patrick is said to have used a hazel rod to drive away the snakes. Irish emigrants often carried a piece of the wood to America to keep them safe, while an old tradition holds that anyone carrying in their pocket hazelwood cut at midnight on May Eve will never fall into a hole, however drunk they might get.

The Celts saw hazelnuts as concentrated wisdom. Nine hazel trees that grew around a sacred pool dropped nuts into the water, where they were eaten by salmon, becoming the wisest of all creatures. In one tale a Druid killed the wisest and instructed his apprentice to cook but not eat it. The apprentice licked a splash from his thumb. He would later become the great Irish hero Fionn Mac Cumhaill, often referred to as Finn McCool or McCull ("coll" being the Celtic word for hazel, so "Finn, Son of Hazel").

China celebrates hazelnuts as one of the five sacred foods of the spirits. In England they have a more practical use: carry one against rheumatism or lumbago, carry two against toothache. The pliable young branches made hurdles for sheep and "wattle" for houses, daubed with mud and lime. While hazel has been used in medicine, especially by First Nation American peoples, for cuts, tumours and ulcers, beware: soothing witch hazel lotion is made from witch hazel, or *Hamamelis*, an entirely different species.

Opposite Hazel (*Corylus avellana*) from *Flora von Deutschland* by Otto Wilhelm Thomé, 1885.

163. *Corylus Avellana L.* **Haselstrauch.**

Saule. WILLOW. 𝔚𝔢𝔦𝔡𝔢.

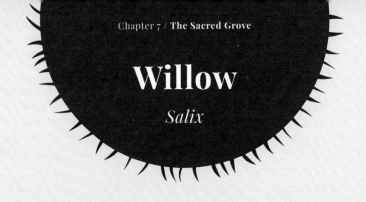

Willow

Salix

There are more than 400 species of willow, growing in a wide variety of terrains. Most are water-lovers and have acquired a suitably "watery" reputation.

Willows were especially important to the ancient Egyptians. Fronds have been found in Tutankhamun's tomb, and the wood was used for camel saddles and vine supports. Willow leaves were prescribed as an appetite stimulant, the seeds incorporated into bandages and combined with hippo dung to make unguents for swellings.

In Hertfordshire, England, willow in the house on May Day averted the evil eye, and in Yorkshire it was hung in doorways to repel witches, but in the same county it was also said to be a witch's tree and if the pussies (catkins) were brought indoors no goslings would hatch. Willow is one of several trees on which it is said Judas hanged himself, yet its fronds were used as substitute palms on Palm Sunday. The tree was said to beget snakes, but its ash drove serpents away.

Willow, and especially weeping willow (*Salix babylonica*), is often associated with sadness and mourning. In England, deserted lovers were said to "wear the green willow". Sometimes a jilted lover would be sent a piece of willow by malicious neighbours, though in Wales a "white stick" made of hazel was usually accompanied by a cruel verse. Sprays of willow were placed on coffins in China as a symbol of immortality, though the famous blue and white "Willow Pattern" plates – and their story

of doomed lovers – are a British invention from the imagination of Thomas Minton around 1780.

Willow is particularly revered in Japan. One famous tale tells of a farmer who objected to a fine specimen being felled for a new temple. That night, under its shade, he met a beautiful woman, who he married. They had a son. The emperor's men returned and cut down the tree. The man came home to find his wife missing and small son crying. He went to the site of the willow; just one branch remained. He carved it into a cradle, which soothed the boy. In a similar tale told in the Czech Republic, the man also carves a pipe which, as the smoke wreathes around his head, takes the form of a beautiful, ghostly woman.

Karyūkai (literally, the Flower and Willow World) is the name for the districts where the geisha entertain. The flower represents the *oiran* or prostitute, whose life is glamorous but fleeting; the willow is the geisha, who bends in the study of her arts and grows sturdy with age.

The ancient physician and pharmacologist Dioscorides recommended willow as a general tonic for pain, and salicylic acid has been used for pain down the ages. Today we know it as aspirin.

Opposite White willow (*Salix alba*) from *Familiar Trees* by George Edward Simonds Boulger, 1906–7.

Apple

Malus

Loved since prehistoric times, apples enjoy
a strange reputation as both humble
and all-powerful.

Apples appear again and again in ancient legend, often as symbols of dispute, beauty, immortality – or all three. In Greek myth, Heracles' eleventh labour was to steal three golden apples from the garden of the Hesperides, the nymphs of the evening. The Trojan prince Paris was given an apple to present as a prize to the most beautiful of three goddesses, a choice guaranteed to upset the other two. When Loki, Norse god of mischief, abducted Idun, goddess of spring, both she and her magical apples of immortality were seized by the giant Thiassi. Many interpretations of the Christian Bible interpret the forbidden fruit Eve and Adam ate after being tempted by the snake as an apple.

Wild crab apples (*Malus sylvestris*) can be found in hedgerows across the world. From them have been bred around 2,000 species, varieties and cultivars. Apple orchards are magical places, cared for by traditions and superstitions attached to the stations of the year.

The noisiest is "wassailing", where people in cider-producing counties fire guns, blow horns, bash saucepans and bellow at the tops of their voices to frighten away evil spirits and awaken the sleeping trees. If a tree blooms out of season, there will be a death in the family. The end of May is a dangerous time for frosts. One story tells of a man who competed with witches for a good crop of apples and lost, leading to "Frankum's night", 19 May, often blighted with late frost. Another legend says St Dunstan traded his soul with the Devil so the frost would only hit on 17, 18 and 19 May.

Some places still christen apple orchards; this should be done on the feast of St Peter, 29 June, or St Swithin, 15 July. Children eating apples before they are blessed will become ill. Another hazard of scrumping are the fearsome guardians of the orchards, Awd Goggie and Lazy Lawrence, who live in the oldest trees.

Harvest time brings apple-related Halloween fun. Bobbing for apples in a barrel of water is purely a game, but girls would peel apples in long strips to find the initial of their future sweetheart, place an "Allan Apple" under their pillows to dream of him, and throw pips into the air for them to indicate where he lived. If pips tossed into the fire popped, the girl was already loved. Some carved suitors' initials into crab apple skins and married the one that lasted longest.

Opposite Japanese crab apple (*Malus × floribunda*) from *Flore des Serres et des Jardins de l'Europe* by Louis Van Houtte, 1845.

MALUS FLORIBUNDA *Sieb.*

en pleine floraison / 463

Wishing Trees

The Karajá and Apinayé people of the Amazonian plateau
tell of a strange Sleep Tree where the great healer and
shaman Uaica learned his craft from Jaguar Man.

D ream trees are not always found in magical, secret glades in the rainforest, however. In the historical region of Silesia in eastern Europe (now mainly Poland), sleeping beneath a humble apple tree would induce dreams of future spouses. Girls also placed an apple under their pillows to dream of their sweethearts, an idea echoed in British divination games at Halloween. In Germany, the blackthorn (*Prunus spinosa*) is known as the Wishing Thorn because it was also used in divination.

The Hindu Kalpavriksha, or World Tree, grants wishes. Some claim it was moved to Indra's palace after humans abused it by wishing evil things on each other. Others say there are five Kalpavrikshas, fulfilling different kinds of wishes, over which the gods (devas) and demigods (asuras) permanently fight. The heavenly trees are said to have roots of gold, trunks of silver, coral leaves, pearl flowers and diamond fruits, but earthly versions include coconut (*Cocos nucifera*), banyan (*Ficus benghalensis),* shami (*Prosopis cineraria*), mulberry (*Morus*) and the Indian butter tree (*Diploknema butyracea*). Similar sacred trees exist in Jainism, Buddhism and Sikhism.

Sometimes a specific tree grants wishes. A now-lost ancient cork oak in Combe, Devon, was said to grant wishes to people who walked three times round it, while pieces of the bark were collected as lucky souvenirs. A more common British custom involved hammering coins into old or felled tree trunks, to relieve invalids of illness and bring general good fortune to all. Scotland saw the far more tree-friendly practice of tying *clooties* (rags) to branches, pre-soaked in water from a nearby well. People still tie ribbons, rags and tokens to trees across the British Isles, sometimes to honour the spirit of the tree, sometimes with a wish, or in the hope that an ailment will wither as the rag rots.

The custom is echoed in Japan. Tanabata or the Star Festival celebrates two stars, former lovers punished for neglecting their work once they were married. Usually separated by the Milky Way, Altair and Vega get to meet during a very short period in July. People write their dreams on long strips of paper called *tanzaku* and hang them in bamboo trees, which grow fast and tall, bearing mortal wishes to heaven.

Many countries now enjoy the custom of writing wishes on pieces of paper and tying them to a "wishing tree", perhaps even to one of a series of regionally native trees that were planted across the world by artist Yoko Ono in 1981 to encourage positivity.

Opposite Ancient mysterious wishing tree at Carn Euny, Cornwall, England.

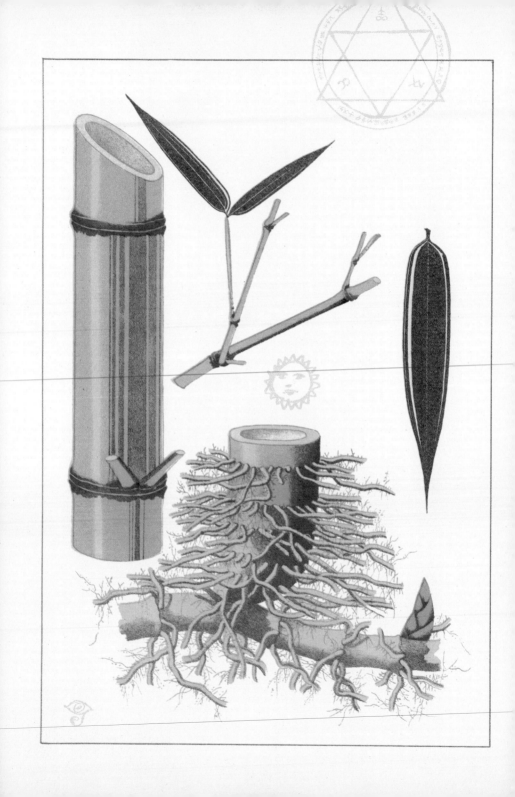

Bamboo

Bambusoideae,
subfamily in Poaceae

Unable to have children, a poor woodsman and his wife
rejoiced on finding a tiny girl inside a bamboo stalk. As she
grew, Kaguya-hime was courted by princes but kept delaying
marriage by giving her suitors impossible tasks.

Eventually she explained she was from the Moon, sent to Earth to learn a lesson, and she wanted to return. Heartbroken, they helped her, and were rewarded with her robe and the Elixir of Life, but they could not bear to take it. The Emperor brought the robe and elixir to Japan's highest mountain and burned them. Smoke has floated from Mount Fuji ever since.

The tenth-century *Bamboo-Cutter and the Moon-Child* is one of many stories centred on the plant's magical qualities. Across the tropical zone, bamboo also grows in cool mountainous places and in damp, mossy cloud forests. It is sacred in many philosophies including Buddhism and Taoism, where its hollowness is a focus for contemplation. Along with plum blossom, orchids and chrysanthemums, it is one of the Confucian Four Gentlemen, representing uprightness, purity and humility, thanks to its strength, rigidity and ability to bend without breaking in a storm.

The world's largest natural bamboo forests occur in southwestern China, where it was introduced to the mortal world by a fairy who stole it from the garden of the gods while the Queen Mother was drunk on the dew of heaven. Associated with long life and immortality, it drives away evil spirits.

For Hawaiians bamboo is sacred to Kāne, the creator god. In Filipino mythology the first humans were made after a bamboo stalk split during a battle between the sky and the ocean, while in Malaysia the first man dreamed of a beautiful creature while sleeping beneath a bamboo. On waking he broke the stem and the first woman was born.

Bamboo is not always auspicious. In parts of India and Nepal, people avoid it due to the ghosts and evil spirits it attracts. Several regions associate it with infertility since nothing grows underneath thanks to its mat of dense roots. In central Nepal, the shadow of bamboo invites death, so planting and harvesting should take place only after sunset.

Yet this immensely versatile plant, the largest member of the grass family, is highly valued. Traditionally used in construction, furniture making and, of course, in food, it is prized for martial arts weapons and is the basis for Malaysian *meriam buluh*, homemade firecrackers. Modern uses include bamboo fabrics, flooring, alcoholic spirits and even bicycles.

Opposite Giant timber bamboo (*Phyllostachys reticulata*) from *Illustrations of the Japanese Species of Bamboo* by Isuke Tsuboi, 1916.

Sandalwood

Santalum album

Prized by the ancient Egyptians for use in medicine,
embalming and ritual fires, the true, white sandalwood has
been grown for more than 5,000 years.

This small tropical tree, sacred to many faiths, has spread from Indonesia to the Juan Fernández Islands of Chile, from Hawaii to New Zealand. This is probably a good thing: over-exploitation has rendered it endangered in its native India. Sandalwood is a hemiparasitic plant deriving enough nutrients from the roots of its neighbours to constantly produce multicoloured blossoms.

Sandalwood oil is extremely expensive, thanks to its multiple uses in medicine, ritual incense, aromatherapy treatments and commercial fragrances. White sandalwood is a slow-growing plant and only becomes suitable for harvesting after 25 years. The older the tree, the more intense the perfume, and the best oil is derived from trees 30–60 years old. Historically, the wood was used for traditional crafts of sandalwood jewellery and sculptures for shrines and, in China, Tibet and Nepal, for temple construction. Today, however, every part of the tree is used to extract oil, including the heart-wood, which is ground down and its essences distilled using steam, making these crafts less common.

In Korean Shamanism, the sandalwood is the tree of life, while for Buddhists it is one of the most popular incenses. For Hindus, sandalwood (*chandana* in Sanskrit) is sacred to Shiva, though the goddess Lakshmi is said to live in its branches. The plant is used in many daily practices of Jains, too, whose monks sprinkle sandalwood powder on followers. Some Jains adorn bodies with sandalwood flower garlands before cremation, while Hindus include a little of the scented wood to funeral pyres. Some Indian Muslims used to place sandalwood censers at the feet of the deceased so their soul might rise to heaven. Zoroastrians often add sandalwood to the *afarganyu* urns kept at the fire temple.

Sandalwood is sometimes made into a fragrant paste, which Hindus use to consecrate ritual tools. Sufis apply the unguent to graves, while some followers of Krishna apply it to their bodies before devotional bathing.

The Arabs introduced sandalwood to the West, using it first to perfume leather saddles in Córdoba, Spain and for medicine. It is used in Ayurvedic traditions for skin problems, while in Chinese medicine it is associated with "kidney yang", which kindles the metabolism, warming the body and making it resistant to stress, and lending sexual potency.

Opposite Sandalwood (*Santalum album*) commissioned by William Roxburgh by unknown Indian artist, 1795–1804. Kew Collection.

Chapter 8:
The Cunning Woman's Stillroom

The popular image of the "herb woman" today usually involves a toothless old crone living alone in the woods, who will probably end up burned at the stake for witchcraft when one of her magic potions goes wrong. While many people did rely on ancient wisdom passed down (largely) by women for their medical needs, herbalists were just as likely to be found in the smartest house in town as a forest cave.

Knowing the properties of every plant meant life or death, and it traditionally fell upon the woman of the house to keep her family healthy. Trees have always been potent weapons in the folkloric armoury and the veil between proven results and magical beliefs has always been thin.

Stillrooms were cool, dry chambers, kept under lock and key, to be used only by the lady of the house, or a trusted servant. Here were stored liqueurs and preserves, spices, coffee, tea and chocolate, along with the family cone of sugar. The stillroom had another valuable use, however, as somewhere to prepare healing balms, poultices, syrups and tinctures.

Medieval and early modern stillrooms bore some similarities to the still-houses of alchemists, natural philosophers who sought to purify base materials into precious metals. "Multiplication" – making gold out of thin air – was illegal in England, banned in 1404 by King Henry IV, but some still secretly worked on the idea. An alchemist's laboratory included athanors (furnaces), grinding mills and vessels in which to distil curious substances in a quest for the Philosopher's Stone, which would grant immortality and freedom from disease. A housewife's (legal) stillroom contained a hearth, pestle-and-mortar and pots and pans, in a quest to ease regular aches and pains.

Family "receipts" (recipes) for tinctures, salves, cleaning agents, pest repellents, flavourings and cordials were handed down from mother to daughter to keep the entire household healthy – from master

Left *The Accomplish't Lady's Delight In Preserving, Physick, Beautifying, And Cookery*, 1675.

Opposite Frontispiece by Nathan Bailey from *Dictionarium domesticum, being a new and compleat houshold* [sic] *dictionary, for the use both of city and country*, 1742. Dated 1736.

to servant, including animals in the barns. Most handwritten "commonplace" books contained far more than food preparation and medicines, including early cosmetics such as a freckle-removing lotion made from distilled elder leaves (*Sambucus*). Walnut juice to cure baldness goes back as far as the Roman writer Pliny. He also suggested that chewing walnuts while otherwise fasting would remedy the bite of a mad dog. There is no evidence that either cure lasted down the ages; family receipt books tended only to keep the recipes that actually seemed to work.

By the sixteenth century, printed housekeeping manuals were appearing. These contained useful recipes alongside others that seem over complicated for general households, or require a long list of exotic ingredients that would be both difficult and expensive to acquire. *The Good Huswifes Jewell* (Thomas Dawson, 1585) includes "approved medicines for sundry diseases" alongside culinary delights such as pancakes, "sallets" (salads) and puddings, but lists expensive ingredients such as dates, frankincense, quicksilver, and "swallowes readie to flie out of the nest". Swallows may have been more plentiful than mercury but needed to be killed before they touched the ground, adding complexity to the exercise. Yet Dawson also suggests tree products, easily procured. Moss gathered from the hollows of a hazel tree staunched wounds, while ash keys, acorn kernels and sloe stones were added to a long list of ingredients that "that will cleane your bladder and leave no corruption therein".

Herbal preparations were suspended in solid

or semi-solid form such as beeswax ointments or "simples" made in advance using preservatives such as alcohol or sugar syrup. Many folk practitioners, however, chose not to entirely rely on medicines made in a cauldron or a stillroom. Humble homes in particular saw little harm and much potential good in ancient superstitions, talismans and good luck charms to guard against both illness and evil spirits.

The family home extended to outhouses, privies and stables, as well as pets and farmyard animals, especially cattle. These were protected with charms, usually garlands, of herbs including rowan (*Sorbus*) and hawthorn (*Crataegus*).

Viburnum lantana, commonly known as the wayfaring tree because of a tendency to grow by country paths, is also sometimes called the "coven tree". Perhaps surprisingly given its alternative folk name, it was often planted by cattle sheds in the seventeenth century to repel witches.

All parts of the elder (*Sambucus*) were useful for food, medicine – and good luck. Hanging dried elder leaves indoors warded off evil, and could magic away warts and vermin, though permission must first be sought from the tree. Birch leaves made an amulet for a baby's cot, while an alder twig in the pocket protected the heart and chest. Carrying acorns was a good general-health talisman across a wide swathe of Europe.

Stillrooms and the related skills that took place therein gradually fell out of favour as (male) university-trained physicians began leaving the secrets of health and beauty to the care of poor relations, women of the village and professional apothecaries. Much was lost or passed on incomplete, later dismissed as "old wives' tales". Some of it does indeed seem a little archaic now. It is unlikely that rotting apples would be used today to cure chilblains and styes,

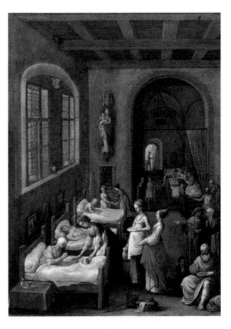

Above *Saint Elizabeth of Hungary Bringing Food for the Inmates of a Hospital*, Adam Elsheimer, c. 1598.

Opposite *Milkmaid after the painting of Gerrit Dou in the Cabinet of Mr. Poullain*, mid-17th century.

as recommended by John Pechey in his *Compleat Herbal of Physical Plants* in 1694, just as no one in Derbyshire literally thrashes chilblains with holly branches to release bad blood anymore.

Yet folk memory is strong and the remedies that worked have remained. In 2021 the world herbal health industry had an estimated worth of $151.91 billion and is projected to grow to $347.50 billion by 2029.[1]

[1] Herbal Medicine Market, Size, Share & Covid-19 Impact Analysis, Fortune Business Insights, July 2022

Myrtaceae
(Eucalypteae)

Eucalyptus Globulus Labillardière.

Eucalyptus

Eucalyptus

One of the great symbols of its home, Australia, there are over 700 species of eucalyptus, ranging from a couple of metres in height to the monoliths that give the Blue Mountains their hazy splendour.

Eucalyptus is named from the Greek *eu* (well) and *kalyptos* (covered), thanks to the tree's unusual flowers that are protected by a cap when unopened, but indigenous people have many different names for it, depending on its size and where it is found, desert to mountain. Most eucalyptus have blue-grey peeling bark. As it sheds in long, curling strips, lighter patches are revealed, giving it a mottled appearance. The tree's red resin sometimes breaks through, giving it its most famous name: the "gum" tree. The varnished gum (*Eucalyptus vernicosa*) is a dwarf variety often classified as a shrub. By contrast, the tallest, a single massive swamp gum (*Eucalyptus regnans*), nicknamed Centurion, in southern Tasmania is currently the tallest flowering tree in the world, measuring 100.5 metres. Wood from the species is sold as "Tasmanian oak" though it bears no relation to *Quercus*.

For aboriginal people, this magical tree provided shelter, medicine and, in the desert, water from its roots. The hard "manna" sap of the ribbon gum (*Eucalyptus viminalis*) is sweet and crumbly, much enjoyed for centuries. Unsurprisingly the tree is considered sacred, a world tree that links the underworld, Earth and heaven. Burning eucalyptus leaves creates a pungent smoke, purifying the air from negative energy. This may be partly due to glands on the leaves that contain an aromatic oil which can be extracted for a number of uses, both medicinal and commercial. Eucalyptus oil is known across the world as an expectorant and for adding to steam to relieve colds and asthma. Its long, hard timber is used for ships, telegraph poles, fences, furniture and railroad ties. Some varieties are ideal for fancy veneers and marquetry.

Eucalyptus enjoys an uneasy relationship with fire. As a species highly adapted to arid climates, wildfires form a part of its lifecycle, and it is quicker to regenerate than most of its competitors. This has led to theories that eucalyptus may have evolved its oil to encourage fire, to clear the forest floor of competitors. There is certainly much we still do not know. Recently scientists discovered microscopic levels of gold in the roots and leaves where the plant had ingested the metal, decided it was a toxin and begun the process of exuding it through its leaves. There is too little to excite a gold rush, though it proves there are tiny amounts of the ore deep in the ground.

Opposite Eucalyptus (*Eucalyptus globulus*) from *Köhler's Medizinal-Pflanzen*, 1887.

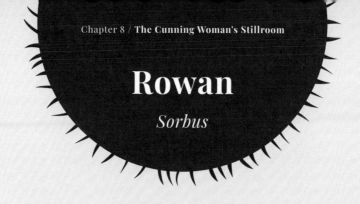

Rowan

Sorbus

Sometimes known as the "lady of the mountains" for its ability to cling to the rockiest crag, rowan is one of the most magical of all trees.

*S*orbus grows in some of the most inaccessible parts of Europe, and the very hardiest specimens, surviving in soilless cracks and arctic temperatures, are known as "flying rowans". Although it has been called a "witch's tree" of evil purpose, most traditions consider the misnamed "mountain ash" to have protective qualities. In Norse myth, Thor was saved from a fast-moving river by grasping a rowan branch, and for centuries new ships included at least one plank of rowan wood, even long after the Northlands were converted to Christianity. Care should be taken, however, as in Iceland it was believed rowans grew by the graves of innocent people who had been wrongfully executed. A plank from such a tree could sink a ship and even a single twig burned in the hearth risked estranging the friends that sat around it.

In Celtic mythology, the first woman was made from rowan (the first man being an ash) and the tree became sacred to Brid, goddess of the arts, healing and midwifery. She was also goddess of weaving, which is why spindles and spinning wheels are traditionally made from rowan wood.

Rowan berries come in bright clusters of oranges and reds that are late to maturity and therefore a valuable food source for animals and birds in late winter. Each tiny fruit bears a five-point star, resembling a pentagram, a traditional sign of good luck. Sprigs of rowan protected everything from babies' cradles to coffins and were attached to the horns of cattle to keep them safe. Even today it is considered lucky to plant – and extremely unlucky to fell – a rowan tree, especially in Scotland. Perhaps this is because it is also thought of as a plant of the fairies. The Fair Folk were said to treat kindly any children that kept rowan berries in their pockets; it was wise to keep a sprig nearby at Midsummer, to aid escape should one become trapped in a fairy ring.

Rowan berries are most famously used for jelly, eaten with meats and game, but they are high in vitamin C, which may account for their reputation as a folk cure for scurvy. They also featured in remedies for diarrhoea, gargles for sore throats and ointment for haemorrhoids. For most people, however, the rowan is a shining symbol of late autumn days, of bright red berries sharp against a forget-me-not sky.

Opposite Mountain ash (*Sorbus aucuparia*) from *Nos Fleurs: Plantes Utiles et Nuisible* by Matthieu Leclerc du Sablon, 1892

Sorbus Aucuparia. L
Der Vogelbeerbaum.

Chapter 9:
The
Dark
Mirror

The traveller steps from the sunshine into the forest. Almost instantly, shadows seem to form, looming close, blotting out the light and conjuring unbidden images of whatever lies within. They feel "watched". Half-remembered stories swirl through the mind, of ghosts and shapeshifters, spirits and portals to other worlds. Strange folk are said to roam the dark forest, where grow unlucky trees and whispers of the cursed. It would be very easy to get lost here, perhaps for ever.

It is not surprising that stories of haunted forests and strange woodland happenings can be found across the globe. While often interpreted as evil, the dark spirits of the forest usually give only as good as they get.

Scandinavian forests are crowded with strange beings, from trolls and witches to werewolves and giants. In Norway, the word *huldrefolk*, "supernatural beings", derives from the old Norse *huldr*, or "hidden", and often refers to forest spirits. The *skogsrå* goes by many names but usually manifests as a dangerous female spirit haunting mainly Swedish but also Danish, Finnish and Norwegian woods. She may have the top half of a woman, beautiful or otherwise; the lower part of her body could be anything from a rotting tree trunk to furry legs, cloven hooves or a cow's tail. Sometimes she travels via brass skis. The *skogsrå* will seduce men, usually travellers or charcoal burners, rewarding those who consent, punishing those who resist, but generally, if humans treat her and her forest with respect the *skogsrå* has better things to do than harm them.

The *skogsrå* is a manifestation of a Scandinavian concept called *metsänpeitto*, or "forest cover", where the forest itself turns against an intruder. The person may specifically step into *metsänpeitto*, perhaps through something like a fairy ring, or just by stumbling into something, such as a magical stone or a tree stump. Symptoms include the forest falling silent of birdsong or the wind in the trees, a feeling of being suddenly unwelcome, or of being "frozen"

in time or place, unable to speak or move, invisible to would-be rescuers. There are a number of simple remedies or precautions for such events, including spells, incantations, or small eccentricities such as turning an item of clothing inside out, which always baffles supernatural spirits.

In other parts of the world, the sensation is recognized but described differently. *Kodama* are the souls of Japan's most ancient trees, usually manifesting as light-filled orbs, which, like many forest spirits, can be malign or benign according to how they are treated. Anime lovers may recognize *kodama* as the sad-eyed little blobs in the 1997 film *Princess Mononoke*. Less cute, the Aokigahara Forest, the Sea of Trees, on the northern slopes of Mt Fuji, confuses walkers into becoming lost. Some blame large deposits of iron ore beneath the volcanic soil for compasses going awry, but these tragic woods have more recently become known as a destination for suicides. Ghoulish reports of *yurei* (ghost) screams have only added to a serious problem for mental health workers.

In an increasingly urbanized world, stories of haunted forests have only slightly moved on from ancient tales of trolls and demons. In 1968 a Romanian military technician photographed what he believed to be a UFO hovering over Hoia Baciu in

Right *Trio of Beech and Oak Trees.*
Illuminated at night in a dark woodland.
Peak District, Derbyshire. Jasper Goodall.

Transylvania, giving the wood's mists and strangely twisted trees a new role in daytime TV "paranormal" documentaries. Claims of a portal at a circular clearing where the sighting took place demonstrate how the sands of folklore are ever-shifting. Some who stumble through this invisible gate will never come back; others return years later with no memory of the intervening time, fates not dissimilar to tales of yore where the unwary stepped inside a fairy ring and found themselves in the kingdom of the Gentle Folk.

Sometimes there is no great mystery and the strange character that haunts a forest is human. Don Julián Santana Barrera meant well when he hung a doll he had found in a tree on the Isla de las Muñecas in Mexico as a mark of respect to a little girl he had been unable to save from drowning. Legend says he could not forget her and began hanging more dolls in the woods, believing each represented a human spirit. He continued collecting dolls for 50 years before dying in 2001. The island is now a macabre tourist attraction; the dolls, many of which are missing eyes and limbs, are considered either evil or protective according to the people they affect.

Individual trees are very rarely thought of as wholly dark or evil. Even "funeral" or "witch" trees such as yew (*Taxus*) and blackthorn (*Prunus spinosa*)

have protective qualities, often only acquiring bad reputations with the arrival of Christianity. One plant, however, has no redeeming qualities. *Euphorbia cupularis* is known across Africa as the dead man's tree. Extremely poisonous, its sap burns and emits an irritant vapour. Zulu mythology knows it as *umdlebe*, used by *umthakathi*, individuals who secretly concoct harmful potions and malicious charms. Yet the plant is, according to tradition, only poisonous if disturbed, only bleeds its noxious sap if the outer layer is broken.

Like the *skogsrå* of Scandinavia or the Japanese *kodama*, the dead man's tree will not harm humans if they treat it with respect. Many a folkloric message hidden in a myth or legend chimes with wider, more mainstream ecological beliefs about our forests today.

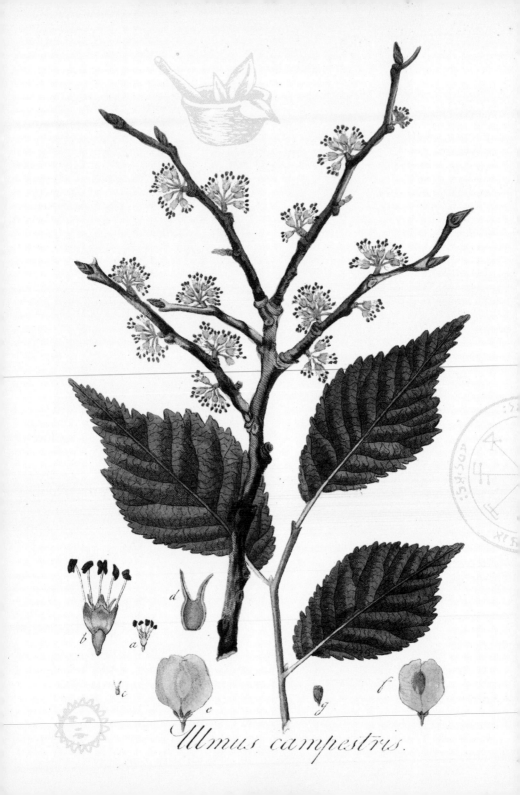

Ulmus campestris.

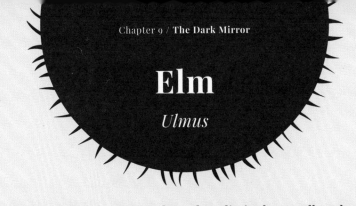

Elm

Ulmus

Mature elm trees are rare these days, limited to small pockets that managed to avoid the latest upsurge of the dreaded elm disease in the 1970s. Yet this elegant tree was once so common that, in England, it was known as the "Warwickshire weed".

It seems darkly appropriate that a tree regularly devastated by a fungal infection spread by beetles should be associated with death. In ancient Greek myth, the musician Orpheus played his harp in despair after failing to release his wife from Hades. Elm trees began to grow, forming a temple for his grief. Later stories muddled the legend and the elm became the tree of Morpheus, the god of sleep. Anyone sleeping beneath it was doomed to endure horrific dreams.

The Romans continued the theme, considering the elm a funerary plant. In Britain, it became a popular tree for coffins, perhaps mostly to do with its water-resistant properties. Elm makes a poor building material because the wood is naturally twisted, but it can withstand damp and even wet conditions, making it ideal for water pipes, bridge bases, cart wheels and shipbuilding. Smaller items such as cheese vats, presses and moulds also lasted longer when made from elm.

Despite its name, wych elm (*Ulmus glabra*), one of several varieties common to Europe, has nothing to do with witches but rather with the pliancy with which it bends. Indeed, witches were said to avoid elm trees, though whether this has something to do with the Norse tradition that woman was formed from an elm (man was created from an ash) is debatable.

The slight bend in elm wood, combined with its pliability, has been exploited for roof beams by barn-builders and by medieval Welsh archers for their longbows, unlike their English counterparts who swore by yew. Dyers prized the tree for its yellow hues, while apothecaries made elm-bark tonics for colds and sore throats, or to treat burns.

In the Channel Islands it was considered safe to sow barley when elm leaves showed, while, in the Midlands, broad beans should be planted before elm leaves are bigger than an old penny.

Elm is not a forest tree; it is most often seen in hedgerows. It could grow to 30 metres in height and live for 100 years but rarely manages this feat. As soon as a sapling reaches a certain maturity, disease attacks. It has killed thousands of trees, including the famous Dancing Elms of Devon and the "Lungs of London", three venerable elms in Hyde Park so beloved that the great Crystal Palace, built for the 1851 Great Exhibition, incorporated the trees into its design.

Opposite Wych elm (*Ulmus glabra*) from *Flora Batava* by Jan Kops, 1822.

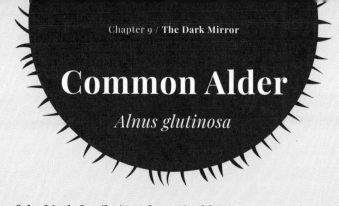

Common Alder

Alnus glutinosa

Part of the birch family (Betulaceae), alder is a swamp-loving tree, making its wood highly resistant to being waterlogged. Diarist and dendrophile John Evelyn noted in his 1664 masterpiece *Sylva* that the great Rialto Bridge in Venice was supported on alder piers.

In ancient Greek myth, the Heliades, daughters of the sun god Helios, were devastated by the loss of their brother Phaeton, who had died trying to drive his father's chariot across the sky. After four months of mourning, the gods took pity on them and turned them into amber-oozing trees. Some accounts say these were alders, others poplar trees. Mythology is never a precise science.

To the Celts, the alder was a symbol of balance between male and female – similar to the yin and yang energies in Chinese philosophy. This was largely due to its being monoecious, bearing both pendulous, yellow male catkins and their green, conelike female equivalent on the same branch. Irish folklore suggests that the first man was created from an alder, but more often the tree is associated with the fairies. Woe betides anyone who chops down an alder, for even as its damaged wood turns from pure white to blood red, the Gentle Folk will burn down the house of the cutter.

This is a shame, as the wood is extremely useful, both practically and spiritually. Associated with war and death, perhaps thanks to its violent colour when cut, alder was sometimes made into shields. An opponent's hatchet, when buried in its soft wood, was difficult to remove, giving the shield bearer an advantage. Alder woodlands or "carrs" were considered mysterious, spiritual places, not least because of the tree also being allied with images of resurrection. In Austria it was even thought alder wood could bring the dead back to life.

Alder wood was good for anything that habitually got wet, such as milk pails, pipes and marshland causeways. Indeed, it was only truly durable if kept wet. For quick use, however, it also made fine charcoal and gunpowder, so became a favourite tree for coppicing. In many places, including Britain and Normandy, alder was used for wooden clogs and shoe heels. John Evelyn suggests that applying the leaves to the sole of the foot refreshed weary travellers.

Alder flowers yield a useful green hue to the dyer's palette, while scholars once made ink from the fruit and bark. In the Peak District of England alder is used in well-dressing, the traditional ornamentation of springs, while anyone who carries the female catkins or "black knobs" in their pocket may be confident they will never suffer from rheumatism.

Opposite Alder (*Alnus glutinosa*) from *Flora Batava* by Jan Kops, 1822.

B

A

C

f

g

a

i   h   e   d   c   b

Alnus glutinosa.

The Woodland Pool

The Devil's Pool in Philadelphia, USA is how many people
imagine a forest lake. According to the First Nations
Lenape people the Great Spirit hurled a gigantic boulder
at the Evil Spirit, which landed hanging over a still pond
in deep woodland in the Wissahickon Valley.

The Devil's Pool is a natural basin, but not all woodland lakes are. The Silent Pool in Albury, Britain, is probably an old chalk pit. Legend holds that a lecherous nobleman surprised a woodcutter's daughter as she bathed in the lake. He rode in, forcing the girl into ever deeper water. When the woodcutter found his child's body floating in the pool, he also discovered the man's hat, that of the perennial folklore villain, wicked Prince John.

Woodland pools are often associated with women. They can be wronged innocents like the woodchopper's daughter, playful nymphs such as the ancient Greek *naiads*, or terrifying monsters. Such monsters often start out innocently, like the horrific *rusalki* of Slavic mythology. These are drowned virgins or children who have died unbaptized and in their new demonic guise they entice abusive husbands and faithless lovers to a watery grave. Not all dangerous spirits are female, however. In Norway, the shapeshifting *nøkk* lives in pools and rivers and appears as a white horse or handsome youth to lure unbaptized children and pregnant women to their deaths.

In Hindu mythology, running waters are sacred to the gods, still lakes support evil creatures. Less spelt-out, the idea manifests in other world folklores. Still water can be stagnant, attract insects and disease, and forest bogs seem the natural lair for monsters such as the mortal-munching bunyip of Australian aboriginal lore. A flowing stream, in times before purification plants, meant safe drinking water and spiritual purity. Pools with a spring, and regularly changing water, were magical, and Celts threw valuable offerings into them; many people still throw coins into water for good luck. Flowing water was also a boundary that vampires, witches and ghosts could not cross.

Springs and pools were assigned to individual deities, later incorporated into religions. The hot springs at Bath in Somerset, for example, were sacred to the Celtic goddess Sulis, remodelled by the Romans as Sulis Minerva. Christianity brought a wholesale takeover, turning "sacred" springs "holy". Many were dedicated to the Virgin Mary as "lady" wells; stewardship of others was assigned to various saints, many of whom also bestowed healing through the waters.

The boulder that the Great Spirit hurled into the Devil's Pool, Philadelphia, still lies where it landed, though, alas, the Evil Spirit lives on in the trash left by careless tourists. We are, perhaps, our own worst monsters.

Opposite *The Bathing Pool* by Hubert Robert, c. 1777.

Groningen, J.B. Wolters. Chromolith v. Emrik & Binger.

TAXUS BACCATA VAR. FASTIGIATA Loud.

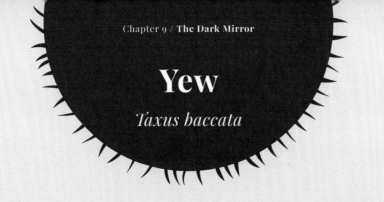

Yew

Taxus baccata

Yew is a tree of mystery, not least because there is no way to tell how old any given specimen may be. Even its name is strange. Dr Johnson thought it might come from the Anglo Saxon *iþ* or Welsh *yw*. If it does, it is the only British tree with a Celtic name.

Dark, spreading, poisonous, the tree has been associated with death since antiquity. The ancient Greeks and Romans considered yew a funerary tree, to be grown on tombs and the gates of graveyards, sacred to Hecate, goddess of entrance ways, witchcraft and the Moon. Nearly every part of the plant is poisonous. Julius Caesar wrote how people he had invaded in the Basque, Gaul and Germania regions, drank yew-root potions to commit suicide or euthanize loved ones rather than submit to the pain and shame of execution.

Yew leaves continued to be used in funerary rituals across Europe, especially within Celtic beliefs. The Druids drew a more positive picture of one of their most sacred trees: that the yew represented eternal life thanks to the tree's habit of sending out drooping branches that rooted as they touched the ground.

Folk memories trickled down the centuries to warn those sleeping under a yew tree that they risked death. Even its shadow was dangerous, though in the Spanish Cantabrian mountains yew was thought to repel thunderstorms. Shepherds built their huts in its shelter, made wattles, clappers and cowbells with its wood, and even used its poisonous qualities as an abortifacient for ailing livestock. Elsewhere the same properties were used more nefariously, as the ingredients for deathly potions. Macbeth's three witches famously threw "slips of yew, silver'd in the moon's eclipse" into their bubbling cauldron.

It is often said that the yews growing in churchyards predate Christianity and some churches were built on popular pagan sites. Practices such as including a sprig of yew in a shroud also seem to continue from earlier beliefs. It is less true that yew roots "thrive" on corpses, or soak up poisonous emissions from rotting bodies, another ancient belief. Other people suggest that churchyard yews may just have been lucky in surviving when their compatriots outside the consecrated boundaries were felled in their thousands to make the most powerful hand weapon of the Middle Ages: the longbow.

Opposite Yew (*Taxus baccata*) from *Neerland's Plantentuin* by C. A. J. A. Oudemans, 1865.

Just as oak forests were felled to build ships, vast quantities of close-grained yew wood went into the English longbow, feared across Europe, scourge of the Hundred Years War. In 1349, Edward III decreed that every able-bodied man must learn and practise archery rather than indulging in football or cock-fighting. The law was strengthened by Henry VIII in 1511, insisting that every man must practise longbow and have a bow and arrow permanently ready at home. This meant a lot of yew wood, and although archery went out of fashion with firearms, the seventeenth-century diarist John Evelyn was concerned about the decline of yew forests.

Luckily the ancient superstition begun by the Romans, never to include yews in ornamental gardening, were changing, not least thanks to the tree's dense growth patterns and ability to resprout from old wood, which made yew hedging perfect for formal boundaries, mazes and topiary.

Some of the world's most extraordinary and ancient trees are yews, but it is impossible to know just how ancient they are. In Britain, the Fortingall Yew has been growing in a churchyard in the Scottish county of Perthshire long enough for a local legend to claim Pontius Pilate was born in Fortingall and played under the tree's branches. Its age is as confusing as the reasons why the village would want to be associated with a Roman official who famously washed his hands of Christ's fate. It is claimed that the Bleeding Yew of Nevern in Pembrokeshire drips blood (actually an anomalous crimson sap) in sympathy with the Crucifixion, though others say it commemorates the hanging of an innocent monk. Similarly, we just cannot know how old the gnarled giants of the great Kingley Vale yew forest in West Sussex may be. Even comparatively young yews can look surprisingly venerable. The problem lies in the way yew regenerates, by sending out branches which take root, leaving older trunks to rot. The specimen's core becomes hollow, with no tree rings for dendrochronologists to count.

Snot gobbles, snotty gogs and snotterberries are just three of dozens of mucus-related folk names for the yew's bright scarlet berries. These flashy, fleshy casings are the only part of the yew that is not seriously toxic, but neither are they tasty to humans. The Greek physician Dioscorides noticed that the berries gave humans diarrhoea and that little birds choked to death on them, but he was only partly right. Writer Richard Williamson, sometime warden of Kingley Vale yew forest, relates how he watched a fieldfare gobble up vast quantities of fruit until it vomited a small pile of 30 seeds now nicely prepared for germination along with some accompanying "manure". The bird then resumed its yew-berry frenzy in "an attack of sheer greed", joined by its friends "like children confronted by bowls of trifle and jelly". Oh, yes, the yew tree has all of us in its thrall.

Opposite Yew (*Taxus baccata*) from *Flora von Deutschland in Abbildungen* by J. Sturm, E. H. L. Krause, K. G. Lutz, 1900–7.

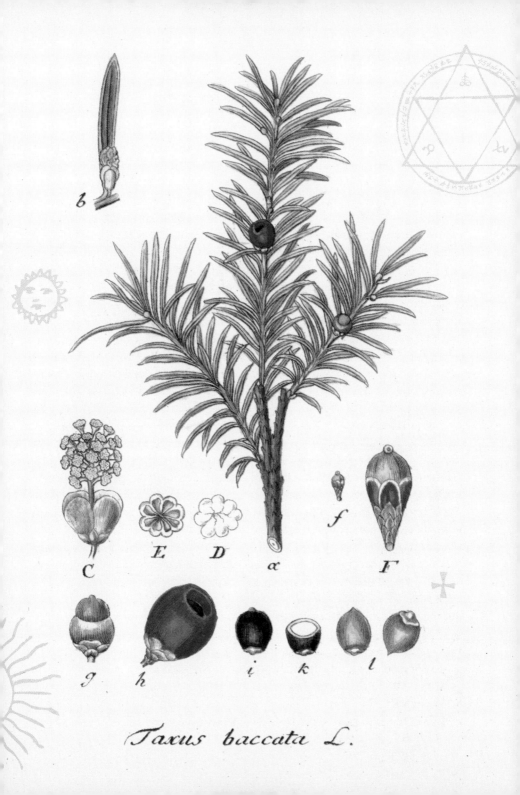

Taxus baccata L.

The Witch's Forest

Most of us first meet a witch in fairy-tale forests,
perhaps as a kindly old woman who soon
reveals her true colours. Historically, witchcraft
continued the pantomime-villain image into real
life, as the enemy of the Christian church.

In medieval and early modern Europe witchcraft was considered synonymous with curse-making, invoking magic to evil ends. In some parts of the world, it still is. Individuals were – and, tragically, still are – accused of devil-inspired sorcery, cast out, and even, occasionally, murdered. "True" stories, once investigated, however, reveal more about the tellers than their subjects.

What do we really know, for instance, of the prophetess credited with foretelling the fates of monarchs, the Great Fire of London and the defeat of the Spanish Armada? Ursula Sontheil was born in a cave in the Royal Forest of Knaresborough in England in 1448, reputedly during a terrible storm. Her unmarried mother refused to reveal the baby's father and word got around that Satan himself had sired her. Ostracized, Ursula learned herbalism before marrying a Thomas Shipton, only to be accused of having cast a wicked spell forcing him to wed her. The rumours did not die when he did a couple of years later. Understandably, "Mother" Shipton became a woodland recluse, but now the same people who had mocked her came with ailments to be cured and to hear her prophecies. Her name has lasted longer than any of theirs.

Slowly, the image of witchcraft morphed from "enemy of the Christian church" into something more neutral, often by public demand. The Harz Forest in Germany has one of the most famous witch festivals in the world, but it has little to do with the saint that Walpurgisnacht is named for. St Walpurga's feast day was intended to replace the popular pagan festival of Beltane, but her festival was merely embraced into the fun and has been synonymous with Hexennacht (witch-night) for centuries. The poet Goethe immortalized it as a famous scene in *Faust*, where the witches dance on Brocken Mountain, inspiring woodcuts, paintings and even a rock opera. The peak is also famous for a strange optical illusion, the Brocken spectre, where the sun shines behind a rock climber who is looking downwards into the mist that clings to the forest 300 days a year. The mysterious shadow of a "giant" is spookily projected onto the tapestry of conifers in a ghostly, rainbow-like glow.

Opposite A wood engraving made in 1892 of Sarah "Granny" Good, a witch executed in Salem, Massachusetts in 1692.

By the twentieth century, witchcraft had, in Europe at least, acquired a softer aspect. Legend tells that Lammas Eve, 1940, a group of witches met by an ancient tree called the Naked Man, deep in the New Forest. At midnight, they raised a "great circle" and invoked a full magical assault on the mind of Adolf Hitler, repelling him from British shores. "Operation Cone of Power" was the latest incarnation of an old tale. Similar stories had seen Sir Francis Drake joining sea witches at Devil's Point, Plymouth to repulse the Spanish Armada; another group was said to have forced back Napoleon Bonaparte in the early nineteenth century. "Operation Mistletoe" tells of a ritual performed in Ashdown Forest, Sussex in 1941, because it was known that the German High Command had an interest in the occult.

It is hard to believe such rites did happen, but the tale speaks to us of how magic has progressed, from being feared as the incarnation of evil to a force for communal good. The stories are told by Gerald Gardner, known by many as the father of modern witchcraft. A former civil servant, Gardner joined a New Forest coven in the late 1930s and went on to mould and publicize the religion known as Wicca, one of the foremost groups within neo-paganism.

Modern witches still gather in forests (although they also meet elsewhere, not least in each other's homes). It is the obvious choice: a place to focus on the natural world, to harness cosmic energies as a powerful weapon for the greater good. Their "tools of the trade" also come from trees, though horrifying medieval woodcuts of witches flying on broomsticks could be considered the early-modern equivalent of click-bait. In a time when most people could not read, printers included a couple of saucy illustrations of witches, familiars and devils to add spice to much less sensational text. It is far more likely that the traditional besom – birch-twig bristles attached to an ash-stave handle with willow strips – was used in ancient times much as it is today, for ceremonially cleansing a space before performing magic or rituals.

Wands, used to focus magic and for divination, are traditionally made from a variety of woods, chosen according to the powers with which each tree is associated. Classic choices include birch (*Betula*) for new beginnings, hazel (*Corylus*) for wisdom, elder (*Sambucus*) for learning and rowan (*Sorbus*) for magical protection. Blackthorn (*Prunus spinosa*) is more often associated with death and blasting. Personal connection with the wood is the most important thing to consider when choosing a wand; even driftwood may speak to some. Each individual should create their own set of wands, offering appropriate respect and thanks to the trees.

Opposite *Baba Yaga* illustration by Ivan Bilibin for *Vasilisa the Beautiful*, 1900.

The Haunted Forest

The dark serenity of a forest can be overwhelming;
it is unsurprising that many of the world's most
memorable ghosts live within the wild wood.

The Wild Hunt is one of the most pervasive woodland motifs. According to many legends, this ghostly party chases through the forests of most European countries, variously known as the "furious army", the "terrifying ride", the "Green Huntsmen" and the "*Åsgardsreie*". It chases various mythical creatures, accompanied by demonic hounds, led by a range of legendary figures – from the Norse god Odin, the Irish giant Finn McCool and the Norwegian witch Guro Rysserova to King Arthur of Britain, Gronveld the Danish Green Huntsman, riding with his head under his arm, and the evil Comte Arnau of Catalonia, condemned to ride for eternity, his flesh constantly devoured by flame. Some say the Wild Hunt predicts disaster. Humans are warned to avert their eyes, should they be trampled underfoot or themselves swept into the chase.

Dozens of forests around the world play host to ghosts, ancient and modern. Pine Barrens, New Jersey, has boasted its own Jersey Devil for more than 250 years, complete with wings, goat's head and hooves. Poor Amy Dudley, first wife of the Earl of Leicester, mysteriously broke her neck falling down the stairs in 1560 and now haunts the Forest of Wychwood in Oxfordshire, England. The tall straight pines, mountain mist and eerie silence of Dow Hill Forest or Kurseong, near Darjeeling make for India's most haunted hill station. Woodcutters report the distinct feeling of being watched or followed, while sightings of a headless young boy and a woman in grey sit uneasily with unnatural deaths, whisperings and footsteps out of termtime at the woodland Victoria Boys High School. In Transylvania, a clearing in Hoia-Baciu woods is said to be a portal through which any who enters will not return.

Yawata no Yabushirazu in Japan is so notorious for people being *kamikakushi* ("spirited away") that the small forest of moso bamboo (*Phyllostachys edulis*) is synonymous with "maze" or "labyrinth". Theories abound. Could the alleged disappearances be the work of a samurai's ghost? Might the forest contain a bottomless pit, leak poisonous gas, or be haunted by a *kitsune*, or fox spirit? So seriously are the claims taken that the sacred site is heavily fenced-off and access strictly forbidden.

Opposite An illustration from *Old French Fairy Tales* by Virginia Frances Sterrett, 1919.

Above The Leshy, a deity of the forests in Slavic
mythology with the ability to shapeshift.

Sometimes spirits more generally haunt the wooded places of the world, such as the Leshy of Slavic mythology, a shapeshifting humanoid who is either evil or benevolent according to mortals' attitudes to the forest. The Nang Tani of Thailand is a young female spirit who haunts clumps of wild banana trees. She is most often seen hovering above the ground at the full moon, her skin pale green, her body fading at the waist.

Occasionally, individual trees gain a reputation for a ghostly tenant. A majestic 250-year-old cedar in Caterham in Surrey is said to have been the execution site of a witch, who cursed anyone that spoke while passing beneath it. The tree's ghostly population now includes a little girl, a nun and a monk. Some passers-by still purportedly hold their breath to avoid joining them.

Saddest of all, however, is the Sea of Trees at Aokigahara in Japan, northwest of Mount Fuji. The forest has played tragic host to more than 500 suicides since the 1950s. Some say that vast underground deposits of iron ore render compasses unusable, causing walkers to take wrong paths and become lost, hearing the spirits of the lost whisper through the night.

The haunted forest should not be confused with a ghost forest, a scientific term for a patch of trees turned to skeletal stumps by salt from rising oceans. Trunks stripped bare of bark protrude from newly made saltmarsh, which itself will eventually turn to open sea as the waters rise. Coastal forests turning to saltmarsh can be a natural process, and such marshes provide wildlife habitats and a buffer against shoreline erosion, but the speed with which ghost forests are appearing in modern times could be considered far more unnerving than any folk tale of demons, goblins or phantoms. Studies made in America show vast stretches of saltmarsh that were once woodland along the Atlantic coast, but ghost forests threaten all the low-lying places of the world including Mexico, Vietnam, Bangladesh and Italy.

Progress of the ingress depends on weather patterns, with hurricanes, droughts, forest fires and human intervention all causing damage at different rates. Scientists are still trying to work out how this will affect us in the future.

Chapter 10:
Trees
of
Hope

From the moment the dove brought an olive branch to Noah, proving the Great Flood was receding and that God had forgiven humans their failings, trees have been symbols of regeneration, resilience, and perseverance. As modern life brings war, pestilence and climate change, trees remain potent talismans of hope in an uncertain world.

Gnarled and twisted, the Great Basin bristlecone pines (*Pinus longaeva*), found high in the western American mountains, are living embodiments of the term "survivor".

The oldest, Prometheus, is over 4,500 years old, but in some ways, these trees were always meant to endure. Others, still venerable, still hardy, but much younger, could be considered more remarkable for their having survived against the odds.

Sometimes those odds are nature-made. Forest fires, lightning strikes and storms fell thousands of trees each year. Some develop extra deep roots against the winds and dry, resinous bark to withstand heat, or regenerate/reseed quickly after natural disasters. Others seem almost miraculous in their survival against disease. Hope for elm and ash, for example, lies with individual specimens that seem to show a natural immunity to elm disease and ash dieback, though some have managed to stay healthy thanks to natural shelterbelts and human intervention, not least a particularly fine collection of rare species of elm in Brighton, England.

Climate change and deforestation have brought about the extinction of hundreds of species, but even here there is hope. The extraordinary wollemi pine (*Wollemia nobilis*) was thought extinct for two million years until a small colony was discovered in the Australian Blue Mountains in 1994. While it remains critically endangered – there are just 100 known trees, hidden in a secret sandstone grove somewhere in Wollemi National Park – its survival is still good news.

Particularly moving are the trees that have survived literally anything humans can throw at them. After the devastating A-bomb dropped on the Japanese city of Hiroshima in 1945, six ginkgo (*Ginkgo biloba*) discovered just 800 yards from the explosion's epicentre threw out new shoots just a few weeks after the blast. Each Hibakujumoku (Survivor Tree) is marked with a name plate and revered as a symbol of new hope in the darkest times.

In a similar miracle, an American elm (*Ulmus americana*) growing in a parking lot across from the

Above A dove returning to Noah's Ark with an olive leaf after the flood in an illustration from *A Child's Story of the Bible* by Mary A. Lathbury, 1898.

building destroyed in the Oklahoma City Bombing, appeared to have died alongside the 168 people who lost their lives on 19 April 1995. Its limbs were blown away, its trunk was encrusted with blast debris and black from fire. Yet this Survivor Tree has thrown out fresh shoots and still serves as inspiration to a grieving city. More recently the stump of a severely burned callery pear (*Pyrus calleryana*) was unearthed by workers clearing rubble after the 2001 World Trade Center attacks. Despite its only sporting a single living branch, a horrified American nation placed much store on its survival. The injured tree was taken to the Arthur Ross nursery in the Bronx where it received intensive care and was returned to Manhattan in December 2010 as part of the 9/11 Memorial and Museum. All of these remarkable trees have yielded seeds and cuttings, which have been sent around the world as ambassadors of peace between nations.

In 1918, the British Government issued a pamphlet, *Roads of Remembrance as War Memorials*, suggesting the improvement of highways by planting avenues with trees "of exceptional dignity and beauty" as permanent memorials to the fallen of the First World War. The idea spread to Canada, the US, Australia, New Zealand and Ireland. Memorial glades and arboretums continue the idea, and trees are often chosen rather than, say, granite headstones, perhaps because a living thing will always bring more joy than cold rock.

Sometimes trees are even planted as memorials to trees. Outside Charing Cross station in London stands an English oak (*Quercus robur*). At nearly 35 years old it is still a sapling and few stop to glance at the plaque it bears. Eighteen people lost their lives on the night of the Great Storm, 16 October 1987; had it occurred by day, the toll would have been far higher.

Above The "survivor tree" in bloom at the World Trade Center site in New York City in 2018.

Britain woke up, however, to a new world, denuded of 15 million trees, commemorated by the Storm Tree.

These stories may seem to have little to do with mythology and folklore, yet they could be called legends in action. Each of the incidents memorialized becomes part of the patchwork of tales people tell each other, embroidered with the passion of lived emotion. Planting a tree is an expression of optimism: in the time in which we grow old and die, they may not even have reached maturity. We plant trees to mark important events. Russian Soyuz spacecraft crews, like their predecessor Yuri Gagarin, add a sapling to the Avenue of the Cosmonauts before every space flight.

Birch

Betula

Many believe the birch was one of the "pioneer" trees that colonized newly exposed land as the glaciers of the last ice age receded. It is often still the first tree to take root on virgin ground, heralding a new forest.

Birch is the first symbol in the early medieval Ogham alphabet, representing the number one. Babies' cradles were traditionally made from birch. While in some traditions, it is associated with death, it may also represent rebirth. In Siberia, the clothes and grave of a dead man were brushed with birch twigs to rid them of evil. Sometimes a birch tree planted would also be planted at the graveside.

The tree was said to remain small because it had never got over the shame of being used to beat Christ. In more recent times, to get "the birch" meant corporal punishment for schoolchildren, criminals and the "insane". The rod was not always a single cane, neither was it necessarily made solely from birch, but a variety of flexible, stripped twigs; hazel was considered most painful. In Scandinavia birch switches stimulate the blood during saunas.

The tradition of decorating churches with birch branches on Whit Sunday appears to have once been widespread in Britain, though it is unclear why. One report, in Philip Stubbs's 1583 *Anatomie of Abuses*, talks of young men and women disappearing off into the woods to spend the night in "pleasant pastimes" before innocently returning with birch branches for the church. Writer and botanist Roy Vickery notes the custom of birch decoration survives at just one church, St John the Baptist in Frome, Somerset.

Birchwood is versatile and tough, its grain straight and solid, ideal for turning tool handles, toys and bobbins. The leaves were said to be diuretic and antiseptic; birch leaves and sap treated kidney stones, rheumatism and gout, and the bark was applied topically to ease muscle pain. Charms made from birch protected the wearer against lightning, barrenness, caterpillars and the evil eye.

Maypoles were often made from uprooted birch trunks while, in Russia, birch sap was used as a lubricant. Its bark was lit as a torch. The Wild Woman of the Woods (sometimes the Lady in White or Silver) associated with the birch tree, appears in folklore across northern Europe. In one tale she distracts a shepherdess from her chores, persuading her to dance for three days. At the end the girl is rewarded with an apron full of birch leaves that magically turn into silver.

Birch wine, made from the tree's sap, is currently enjoying a revival in Scotland and Russia and on internet recipe pages.

Opposite Downy birch (*Betula pubescens*) from *Flora Danica* by Georg Christian Oeder, 1877–83.

1   2   3

The Giants

Giant Redwood
(*Sequoiadendron giganteum*)
and Coastal Redwood
(*Sequoia sempervirens*)

While often considered interchangeable, these two
skyscrapers are subtly different. Both have inspired awe,
respect – and some dirty tricks.

In 1852, famous plant hunter William Lobb was in San Francisco, packing up to go home, when he attended a meeting where fellow hunter Dr Albert Kellogg introduced a Mr A T Dowd who had "discovered" a new, massive conifer. Dr Kellogg told the meeting he was close to announcing it to the world; all he needed to do was collect a couple more samples to register the species as "Washingtonia" in honour of the first president of the United States.

Lobb immediately set out to get there first. Following Dowd's descriptions, he found Calaveras Grove, where he collected samples, seeds and a cross-section of trunk, then hot-footed it back to Britain. On Christmas Day 1853, the *Gardeners Chronicle* announced Mr William Lobb's new discovery: the "Wellingtonia", named for the Duke of Wellington.

After many years of acrimony the row was settled by giving the tree a Latin name: *Sequoiadendron giganteum,* though both countries persist in calling it their own names.

Giant redwood is often confused with its cousin, the coastal redwood (*Sequoia sempervirens*), and both trees do share similarities, not least a distinctive cinnamon-red bark and a seeming desperation to touch the heavens. Both are native only to California, but while the coastal redwood prefers the marine fogs along the northern Californian coast, giant redwoods enjoy the dry heat on the western slopes of the Sierra Nevada mountains. Coastal redwoods, which live up to 2,000 years, tend to be taller than their cousins, but giant redwoods live longer and are bulkier, earning them the title of the largest trees in the world. "General Sherman", a *Sequoiadendron giganteum* weighing in at 1.9 million kilogrammes and standing 84 metres tall, is the world's largest living tree.

First Nations people have various stories about both species. The redwoods, some say, were village elders to Coyote, the creator, in the times when all plants and animals were people. The Tolowa Nation talk of a giant redwood standing at the centre of the world, while the Tule River Tribe consider sequoias to be Ancient Ones, deserving of the highest respect.

Opposite Giant redwood (*Sequoiadendron giganteum*) from *The Pinetum Britannicum* by Edward James Ravenscroft, 1863–84.

Sequoia wood provided homes and canoes. The leaves could be made into a poultice for earache, but First Nations people only ever used fallen and dead wood. Cutting down a tree was considered an act of violence. This was not a view shared by the settlers. On top of logging on a grand scale, wanton acts of tree violence included the famous Wawona Tunnel in Yosemite, which had a road cut through its trunk in 1881 as a tourist attraction. It collapsed in 1969. Sequoia National Park was created in 1890, the first to protect a living organism.

Today it is estimated that between three and five per cent of California's original two million acres of redwood forest survive.

Opposite Giant redwood (*Sequoiadendron giganteum*) from *Curtis's Botanical Magazine*, 1854.

Below *The Mariposa Grove of big trees, California* (*Sequoiadendron giganteum*) by Marianne North, Kew Collection, c.1876.

Fitch del et lith Vincent Brooks Imp.

II,1   131.Oleaceae

Olive

Olea europaea

Poseidon challenged Athena to a battle, their prize the greatest
Greek city of all, the judges its inhabitants. The sea god sent
the people a magnificent waterway filled with fresh drinking
water but Athena knew what they really wanted.

The goddess of warfare also ruled wisdom. She struck her staff on the ground, from which sprang an olive tree, and easily won the competition. The grateful citizens named their city after her: Athens. They lit her temple, the Parthenon, with olive oil lamps and marked boundaries with her trees. The hero Heracles wielded a club of olive, imbuing it with strength.

The olive spread from Iran, Syria and Palestine to North Africa and the Mediterranean basin around 6,000 years ago, where it became one of the first cultivated trees. Stones have been found in Egyptian tombs.

The Greeks adopted the olive as their own. They too planted it near sarcophagi, as a symbol of eternal life. One of the longest living trees, a mature olive trunk can live at least 1,500 years. It is said the giant olives growing in the biblical Garden of Gethsemane were already growing when Christ walked there 200 years ago. Radiocarbon dates most to around 1200, but the five largest are hollow, and impossible to test.

The olive has always been associated with peace. Winners were given olive branches as prizes in the original Olympian Games (the rival Pythian Games presented laurels to athletes). Greek farmers burned an olive branch at harvest to ensure a good crop the following year, and brides wore a sprig of olive as a symbol of chastity. Some people just wore sprigs for good luck or good health. A superstition among Italian peasants decided how lucky they would be in the coming year by the colour of the first ripe olive they saw.

For the Romans the tree was sacred to Athena's equivalent, Minerva, and Pax, the goddess of peace. Perhaps oddly, Mars, god of war, is also sometimes depicted with a branch, as the "bringer of peace". Olives appear several times in Genesis, the earliest chapter of the Bible, most notably after the Flood, when Noah sends a dove from the ark to look for signs of land. It eventually returns with an olive branch, symbolizing God's forgiveness. God told Moses to use olive oil for anointing. It lit lamps in the Jewish Tabernacle and, along with bread, wine and water, consecrated oil or "chrism" remains one of the most important symbols in Christianity.

Opposite Olive (*Olea europaea*) from *Flora von Deutschland* by Otto Wilhelm Thomé, 1885.

Further Reading

It is impossible to cover every aspect of folklore, medicine, superstition and custom about trees in a book this size. More than any of the previous titles in this series, it is intended merely as an appetizer, a gateway drug to the joy of folklore and trees.

There are hundreds of books about forests and trees, about folklore and about folklore and trees. Indeed, there are entire books devoted to a single species. I have been grateful for these and the thousands of articles in magazines and online, often on very obscure websites. There are far too many to mention here, but I found the following particularly helpful, and recommend them as a very basic start. I wish you much joy delving into the wonderful, bottomless world of tree lore.

I am a fan of Ruth Binney, especially her "little" books, including *The English Countryside* (Rydon, 2015) and *Plant Lore and Legend: The Wisdom and Wonder of Plants and Flowers* (Rydon, 2016).

Similarly, I will buy anything written and self-published by Chris Howkins. Many of his books focus on specific trees, such as *Rowan: Tree of Protection*, *Elder: Mother of Folklore* and *Holly: a Tree for All Seasons*. His books are mostly out of print but well worth tracking down.

The exceptional Roy Vickery writes (and speaks) superbly on the folk names of plants. *Vickery's Folk Flora: An A-Z of the Folklore and Uses of British and Irish Plants* (Weidenfeld and Nicolson, 2019), is a must-have for all folklorists.

Mark Oxbrow is a Scottish folklorist now based in Australia. I return constantly to his works *Halloween* (Strega, 2001) and *Rosslyn and the Grail* (with Ian Robertson, Mainstream 2006).

Charles M Skinner Lippincott's 1911 *Myths and Legends of Flowers* is as rare as hen's teeth, but it can be found as a print-on-demand and covers world folklore.

Icy Sedgwick usually writes fantasy with a folklore twist. Her folklore blog is marvellous. www.icysedgwick.com/category/folklore/

Lucya Starza writes about pagan magic and modern Wicca. Her books cover poppets to candle magic. Her blog, *A Bad Witch*, discusses all manner of folklore, plant related and otherwise. www.badwitch.co.uk.

I was delighted to delve into the excellent *Druidry* website: www. druidry.org/druid-way/teaching-and-practice/druid-tree-lore.

And...

There are so many wonderful books about trees. I particularly loved Thomas Pakenham's *Meetings with Remarkable Trees* (Phoenix, 1996) and *Remarkable Trees of the World* (Weidenfeld & Nicolson, 2002); Tony Hall's *The Immortal Yew* (Kew, 2018) and *Great Trees of Britain and Ireland* (Kew, 2022); and Richard Williamson's *The Great Yew Forest: the Natural History of Kingley Vale* (Macmillan, 1978).

Opposite *Ancient Hollow Beech Tree at Night.* Backlit with ethereal mist. Buckinghamshire. Jasper Goodall.

Index

Picture credits

The publishers would like to thank the following sources for their kind permission to reproduce the pictures in this book.

All other images are taken from the Library and Archives collection of the Royal Botanic Gardens, Kew.

ALAMY STOCK PHOTO: Antiqua Print Gallery 47; Art Heritage 108; Artefact 138; Artokoloro 40; Chronicle 53T, 53B, 59, 67, 98, 101; Classic Image 14; Classic Stock 46; Keith Corrigan 185; Ian Dagnall Computing 190; Gibon Art 41; Granger – Historical Picture Archive 181; The Granger Collection 105; Heritage Image Partnership Ltd 81, 160; Historic Images 102; Interfoto 54, 97, 165; Montagu Images 137; Painters 12; Susan Poupard / Stockimo 151; Mike Read 34; Science History Images 69; Sunny Celeste 75; Svintage Archive 186; Vicimages 42-43

GETTY IMAGES: duncan1890 117; Hein Nouwens 15; Julius Reque 55

THE METROPOLITAN MUSEUM OF ART: The Cloisters Collection 73; H. O. Havemeyer Collection 139; J. Pierpont Morgan 175

MILLENNIUM IMAGES: Jasper Goodall 169, 201

SCIENCE MUSEUM GROUP: 158

SHUTTERSTOCK: Michael Benard 106; Blaze Pro 64; Carl DeAbreu Photography 191; Stephen Orsillo 111

WELLCOME COLLECTION: 159, 161

WIKIMEDIA CREATIVE COMMONS: 10-11, 26, 27, 28-29, 60-61, 72, 88, 96, 109, 182

Every effort has been made to acknowledge correctly and contact the source and/or copyright holder of each picture. Any unintentional errors or omissions will be corrected in future editions of this book.

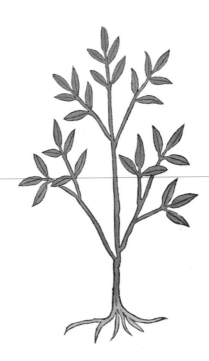